LAST LOOSENING

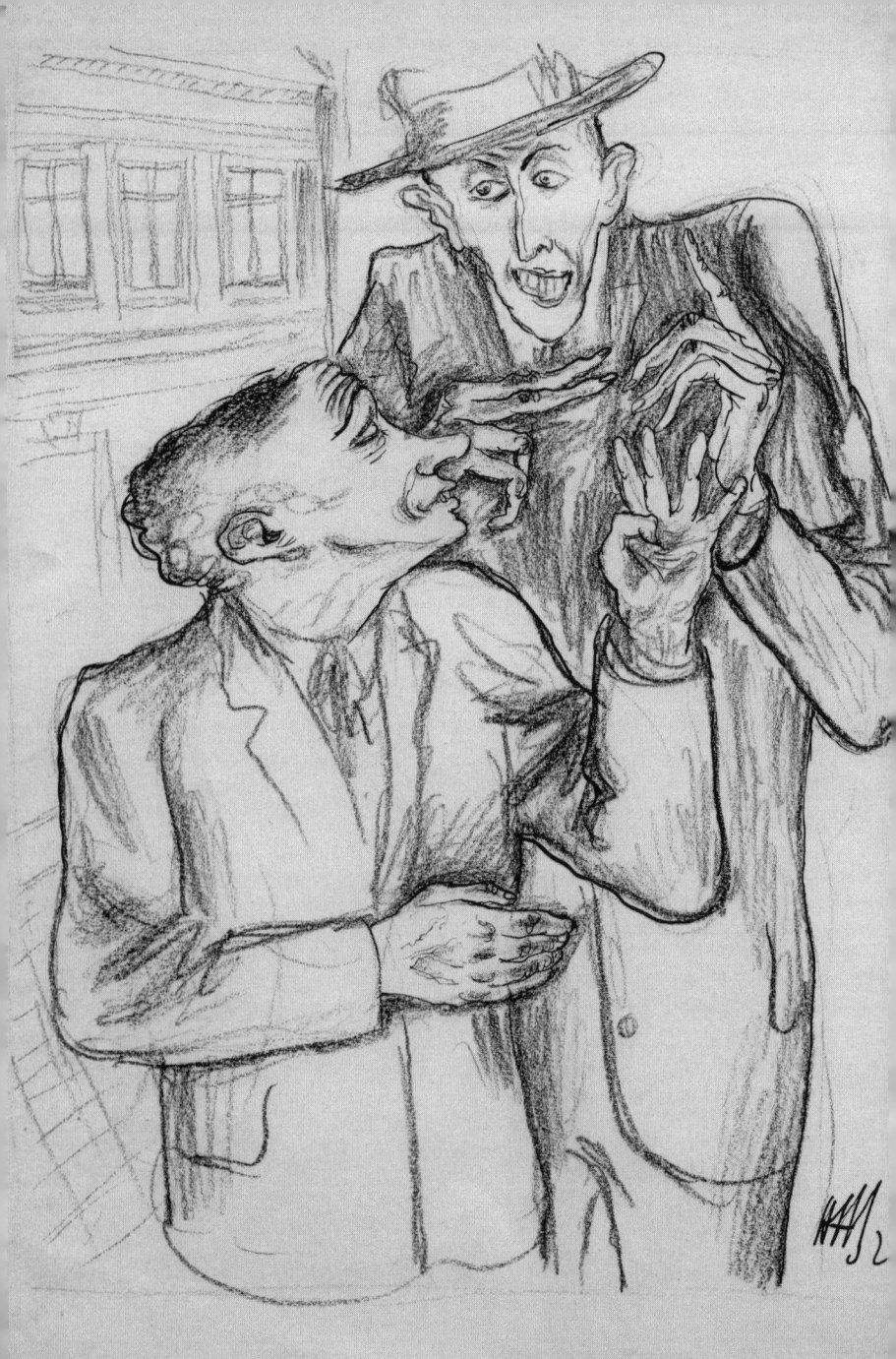

Walter Serner

LAST LOOSENING

A Handbook for the Con Artist
& Those Aspiring to Become One

Translated from the German
by Mark Kanak

TWISTED SPOON PRESS

Prague

2020

ISBN 978-80-86264-45-5
ISBN 978-80-86264-97-4 (ebook)

The translation of this work was supported by
a grant from the Goethe-Institut which is funded by
the German Ministry of Foreign Affairs.

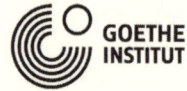

GOETHE
INSTITUT

CONTENTS

To Anton van Hoboken

PART I

THE HANDBOOK OF PRINCIPLES

PREPARATION

Before reading, you should take a lukewarm bath, rest half an hour, then immediately go to an excellent restaurant dressed in your evening best and have yourself served the following dinner:

Portuguese oysters (Pfälzer 1921)
Hors d'oeuvres variés
Trout, buttered
Asparagus, white sauce
Poulet (Chambertin)
Cauliflower au gratin
Pommes frites
Salad
Omelette soufflee
Camembert
Peaches, grapes
Nuremberger Pumpernickel (Lanson brut 1911)
Black coffee
Chartreuse jaune

Take coffee and liqueur in the restaurant, however, only if you're sitting undisturbed. Otherwise you should find a quiet corner in a café or bar and, in addition, straightaway order a Grand Marnier, Ruban rouge, and Cherries Jubilee, letting it sit untouched until the signal to eat is given. At this point, you should light up your preferred smoke and start reading this lesson, pausing for three minutes after each fragment to sip your drink and smoke. After finishing each of the six sections, put the book down and look up at the *plafond*.

It should take you no more than an hour to get through Part I, and it should leave you feeling imbued with an extraordinary energy to take action. Surrender to it only when changing venue, and wait for the signal before putting into play the more important element (a lady).

Anyone who is made miserable by parents, primers, Bible, and bigwigs, and saddled with an inferiority complex, hence not only dreams in those sultry nocturnal hours about bludgeoning that tyrannical pack, but also wallows in grim fantasies about becoming the fortune-seeker of his own body and life, saving up for many months, if no other way is available, so as to be served *this* particular meal before reading, and if having no lady for company, to be able to pay for one. Yet whoever acts contrary to the preparation stipulated herein will so limit the impact of this book that its purpose, which is to loosen you up for good and to make of you what in essence you are, may very well come to utter failure.

If the instructions are followed, however, then this Handbook will have merely proven to be the first adventure, one leading to another, from city to city, from country to country.

Those who have long desired to follow this path may well find pleasure in these pages and the preparation prescribed prior to reading them: a powerful culmination of all that is the body and the brain, intensifying the desire to accomplish new deeds.

---

*(So as not to annoy heavy drinkers, it should be mentioned here that though the quantity to be imbibed is not set, it is advisable to order only half a bottle of each type of wine and to leave a glass from each for the waiter.)

1st Motto:	Each man his own pope!
2nd Motto:	*Non, je ne marche pas.*
	Non, je ne marche plus.
	Mais j'irai peut-être à Canada.
	Chi lo sà?
3rd Motto:	"Your name has nothing to do with it.
	But what is your name, dearest love?"
4th Motto:	(The art-cow went oh so slowly to the stream
	till I busted her behind the ears.)
5th Motto:	*Que les chiens sont heureux!*
	Ils se ....,
	Ils s'.... ... entre eux;
	Que les chiens sont heureux!
	(Ami, ami!)
6th Motto:	His legs astride two beams
	a peacock's feather at the mast,
	so he goes, it makes you weep,
	and with gentle haste,
	who? The pack.
7th Motto:	You've got to have *gumption,* you've
	got to be *strong!*

1. Around a fireball speeds a glob of excrement upon which ladies silk stockings are sold and Gaugins discussed. A truly, thoroughly distressing state of affairs that is nevertheless relative: Silk stockings can be grasped, Gaugins cannot. (Imagine Bernheim as a conjurer biologist). The thousand rastas with their tiny brains and odious observations who serve up aesthetics to erect bourgeois index fingers (O impasto piss?!!) to fix expressions have caused such decrepitude that even today many a lady falls short. (Here, one may reflect three minutes on the psychosis of poorly treated eyesight; primary clinical symptom: underestimation of ladies silk stockings; secondary: digestive disorders).

2. What might the first brain to appear on this planet have done? Presumably it was amazed at its own presence and didn't know what to make of itself and the filthy vehicle beneath its feet. In the meantime, humans have grown so accustomed to their brains they're considered of little importance and hardly even worth ignoring, having made of themselves rastas (at the least: peepshow proprietor; at the most: let's say President of the Senate) and of nature, so unjustifiably beloved, the backdrop to a rather compelling work. This undoubtedly unheroic avoidance of a still insufficiently appreciated dilemma has truly become utterly dull, since it is so predictable (how idiotic personal scales!), though still quite suitable for executing certain procedures.

3. It occurs even to a train engineer at least once a year that his relationship to the locomotive is anything but compulsory and that he doesn't know much more about his spouse than he did

after that steamy night in the Bois. (If I would have said La Villette or Theresienwiese, both relationships would be completely illusory. A tip for aspiring habilittantes: "Concerning topographical anatomy, psychic atmospheric change and the like.") On the other hand, at the Hotel Ronceroy or in Picadilly you may already find it fiendishly unclear as to why just now you're gaping at your own hand and warbling, hear yourself scratching, and love your spittle. This seemingly so serene example offers the greatest potential for the acute feeling of boredom to skip its way along to a thought about its cause. Such lovely moments as these beget the desperado (oh what a sweetie!) who gets up to all sorts of shenanigans as a prophet, artist, anarchist, statesman, etc., in short, as a rasta.

4. Napoleon, such a fine young fellow, asserted most irresponsibly that the true calling of a man was to cultivate the land. And why? Did a plow fall from heaven? Yet *something* must've put *Homo sapiens* on this path, such as the voice of a love-starved woman, I suppose. Well, it certainly wasn't the fields, and after all, herbs and fruits were around back then. (On this point, please consult the German biogeneticists to see if I'm mistaken. As doing this will prove to be quite boring, I am correct.) Ultimately, then: Even Napoleon, who otherwise expressed himself without inhibition in a way that was rather pleasantly refreshing, was at times an athlete of moods. Too bad. Really too bad.

5. *Everything* is, in fact, rastaquouèresque, my dear people. Everyone is (more or less) an utterly airy entity, *dieu merci*. (Quick aside: 10 pfennigs to the clever fellow who can prove to me there is something of late that does *not* arbitrarily scamper around as the norm!) Otherwise, by the way, dying would become epidemic. Diagnosis: rabid boredom; or: panicky resignation; or,

transcendental resentment, etc. (It could be further amplified as you please and elevated to an inventory of all uncharismatic states.) The present routine accounting of the inhabited surface of the Earth is, therefore, merely the logical consequence of a boredom that's become unbearable. Boredom: simply the most innocuous name of all! Let each come up with a more pungent expression for his own inferiority! (A fine subject for a lively game of forfeits.)

6. It is generally known that a dog is no hammock, less so that in refusing to accept this fine hypothesis the daubing fists of painters would droop, and not at all that interjections are the most apt: Worldviews are word salads . . . Sapristi, here the procedure has to be expanded a bit. (Small picture: a light craniotomy!) Thus: all stylists are not even asses. For style is solely a gesture of embarrassment possessing the wildest structure. And since embarrassment (after sleeping on it a bit) reveals itself as the perfect type of self-regret, it is worth noting that these stylists, fearful of being taken for asses, conduct themselves far more deplorably than asses. (Asses have in fact two excellent qualities: they are as stubborn as they are lazy.) The difference between Paul Oskar Höcker, Dostoevsky, Waldemar Bonsels, and Wedekind is revealed solely in the restraint inherent in the aforementioned gesture of embarrassment. Whether one murmurs to me in properly formed trochees or in a torrent of images (all images are plausible!) or, so to speak, expressionistically, that he was feeling ill, but from the moment he had it down in black and white he felt better, or that in fact he felt fine all along (see, see!) yet became ill when he no longer understood it (teremtete!): It is always the same sub-ass effort, a desire to elude embarrassment by giving it (stylized,

ogodogodo) — *form.* Atrocious word! That is: to make out of life, which is improbable head to toe, something probable! To place over this chaos of filth and mystery a redemptive heaven! To fragrantly scent and bring order to this human dungheap!!! Fine thanks . . . Is there a more idiotic image than (ugh!) an ingenious stylizing head flirting with itself during this activity? (By the way: my compliments to the clever fellow who can prove to me that such flirtatiousness is *not* found among these prigheads!) Oh, the too vivid embarrassment that ends with one bowing to oneself! *This* is why (thanks to this, stylized genuflecting) philosophies and novels are slaved over, paintings daubed, sculptures chiseled, symphonies grunted out, and religions established! What ghastly ambition, all the more so because these vain jackasses (and especially in the lands of Central Europe) have utterly failed! It's all hogwash!!!

7. The loveliest scenery I know is Café Barratte near Les Halles in Paris. For two reasons. I met Germaine there, who, among other things, whispered: *"J'voudrais bien être bonne, si j'savais pourquoi."* I spitefully admit: I paled with joy. And then Jean Kartopaitès, who otherwise only associates with gentlemen without stiff collars, abruptly stopped having anything at all to do with me because I was so careless as to drop the name of Picasso.

8. Oh, those dear, white porcelain plates! Because . . . Well this: Formerly people wanted to convey what they claimed was inexpressible, or in fact didn't even have, through painting. (Hurray! As if one could counterfeit a fine, tidy portrait of a vicereine only if unaware that she isn't an armchair!) One might snicker beforehand at the thought of what would become of these daubers if they stopped jacking off with their oil-photos. (Behind the ears:

more girls, please, more girls!) Yet the impressions! So then: *What* is achieved when, after blinking furiously, we make it possible that this potatoglutton sees only a cow, and only *just so* he can pump himself up with the notion that it was *his* cow, a very special cow, in short: *the* one *and* only cow of redemption! Teremtete! Yet the expressions! Ho ho: *What* is achieved by fixing our gaze on what an adjective might accomplish and, having so far failed to provide any sort of orientation, thus a failure if left unpainted? Yet the Cubists, the Futurists! Hey ho: These champions of utterly ultraviolet brushstroking failure did indeed bleat that with — (pah!) — *liberatio* they would descend from the high styleswing (Trapeze kicker! Trapeze kicker! It goes something like this: "We'll eventually get the swing of this embarrassment!"), and yet all they achieved was that not a single chignon started to swing, and worse, the wildest asses arrivisted at a steady gait. (Oh Sagot, mounted by his own spawn! Etc. pp. pp.) Hogwash! Hogwash!! Hogwash!!!

9. In essence, all that was said in Fragment 8, restated for the immature among us as if from a school primer, a superprimer. Yet simply listed here, just to be on the safe side, my dears:

a) Sculpture: rather cumbersome playthings, amplified by metaphysical eyes upturned;

b) Music: a substitute for Pantopon, or Eros. (Long-ago pre-primer!);

c) Lyric poetry: a boy feels stuck in a tight spot. The prescription: ask him whom he's dreaming of and you'll be able to tell him with whom he hasn't slept. (Obviously one is always in a tight spot, yet one shouldn't stay stuck in a C-clamp);

d) Novels and such: These folk talk like they're turning on a skewer, or lately, not at all. A little more sweat needed to achieve success. *Belles lettres!* (Often enough one finds oneself skewered. A Samuel Fischer book, however, is a much too tedious means for establishing the Syracuse–Butterbread–Central Heating airway);

e) drama, tragedy, comedy: The clamp tightens, tensions rise, and the vague suspicion stirs in the public that a cinema is in fact the best second dessert (in the absence of dalliances).

To sum up, my dears: Art was a childhood disease.

10. one never has a thought. In the best case, the thought acts as if it . . . (But there will always be nitpickers!) Every word is a disgrace, mind you! People forever only trumpet sentences of the most circus-like élan across suspension bridges (or also: plants, ravines, beds). A helpful suggestion: Before going to sleep, consider, with the utmost lucidity, the ultimate mental state of a suicide who ultimately would like to bolster his self-esteem with a bullet. But first you have to make a fool of yourself to succeed. A major fool. An appalling fool. An utter fool without equal. A fool so horrendous that everything else is likewise made foolish. So that everyone falls metaphorically on their rumps. And sneezes.

11. Interjections are the most apt. (Oh, those dear, white porcelain plates!) . . . These amphibians and salamanders that think too highly of themselves to be asses must be brought to reason. By driving it out of them. Whipping it out of them! You must tear down this ghastly, larger-than-life, postcard-blue these dim rastas have used to lie to the hi- ho- hu- ha- (sorry?) hea-vens. You must tap your head, lightly yet firmly, against your neighbor's head, as if tapping on a rotten egg (good, good). You must fully roar the utterly indescribable, the utterly unspeakable, intolerably close

that no mongrel would dare go on living so cleverly, but rather more stupidly. So that all lose their reason and regain their heads. You have to shove the percentages, the biblical sayings, the girls' breasts, the pancakes, the Gaugins, the snotrags, the shots, the garters, the toilet lids, the waistcoats, the bedbugs, all the stuff they simultaneously think, do, and are captivated by, so brutally, one after the other, right into their faces so that they're as comfortable with it all now to the same degree of the sole revulsion they felt before. You must. You simply must. Teremtete!

12. Ladies silk stockings are priceless. A vicereine *is* an armchair. Worldviews are word salads. A dog *is* a hammock. L'art est mort. *Vive le rasta!*

II

13. It does no good to prattle on about tyranny . . . What are you to do with your (how to put it?) freedom, eh? Every revolution has been an insurrectionary longing for the more beloved fist (eromasoch). The number of those of age who sneer at all authority is as negligible as the number of despots (crosade), and is entirely inadequate. And so there has never yet been a revolution. Only revolutionaries. Rastas. The year 1789 was the most bungled in history. The solid majority of starving bellies moaned away in front of the Palace of Versailles and intoxicated by the boisterous streets commenced with lopping off heads. Revolution, eh? The hysterical scuffle of organically stunted wannabes. Freedom? A guaranteed minimum standard of living, a guaranteed minor trade, safety from being slapped, and the missus relegated to one quarter sexual gratification so that the man at her side, factory for bureaucrats (soldiers) and miserable glutton, may ripen toward the heavens. Spectacular! . . . Only when this continuous pressure from above abates, the calming knowledge that you need not go on, will everything, yes, *everything,* be all right . . . There really is no point in warbling on about tyranny any longer . . .

14. It could be said that more competent rebels have now clearly advanced more drastic changes. Yet where was the (ha!) — mighty? (O Sophocles, you dour egg dealer!) . . . Freedom! My existence, sovereign? On the contrary: it is powerfully passive, hemmed in from all sides. The great di-do-DTs!!! (And yet quite pleasant . . .) The *whole* (incl. huffing and puffing — express trains) could be enclosed in brackets: Even in related matters of

deception, you tend to watch it when putting something over like this, in fact, you cannot actually feign crawling off somewhere, even with this bracketed grandeur. A yardstick, you who are so measured! You sloops of free will!! You cerebral hoppers!!! Between forceps (smack), birth, and death you hop along with what you had when begot, at times jauntily, at times insipidly, up and down; you hop (yes, yes) — intellectual training, sexual enlightenment (what about with adults?) and similar grandiose absurdities; and you hop along, too (ugh, no!) — freedom, free will . . . bracket-twerps!!!

15. These scumbags, introverted personality types, hard-working arrivistes, etc., jostle to fill, even if stupendously one-sidededly stupid, at best just a small opening (a most desired swinescribbler) in some edition (rubber ball) that quickly closes up again because the others, the airy, so versatile and nimble, rattle away like a quivering weathervane (*"Blow on Bucharest vertically!"*) and by far are in the majority. Fortunately so. Heads, repelling or attracting? The noses they wear repel or attract. So you would be hard pressed to find more idiotic optimists than ri-ra-revolutionaries (every stitch a real snag!). Golgotha was child's play compared to the absolute catastrophe that recently disfigured the face of Central Europe . . . Experience? The long nose we always need to avert if we are not to spontaneously lead ourselves by it. Yet, thoughtless young man, just keep an eye out for that indulgent grin those folks (even Gustl Pufke and, naturally, Thomas Mann) who've enjoyed success (state endorsed nose-leading) are able to spot in their immediate vicinity.

16. Walk right in, gentlemen! Just walk right in! Whatever you haven't seen already won't be seen here, either, but you will see a

menagerie that is certainly something. Truly *worth* a look! Hello:
. . . Whoever uses the ludicrous-positive bustle of the most morose
as stimulus stands up and prophesies a God-system that, in an
attempt to stifle the desperate torment of one's own boredom,
entraps the brain, always roped by suggestion in the noose of a
completely unprovable fundamental assertion (axiom, idea, a
priori tenet, etc., hogwash). Titillated, he amuses himself at everyone's expense, and it is so shameful for the public that such a man
could be so full of himself . . . Another produces a tome covering
final (bum!) — questions and serves it up with an inimitable
expression on his face (one latches onto the hips) — solutions,
hmm . . . Another fellow gets angry about it and becomes churlish
(and not because the situation is insoluble, but because it is a disgrace) and a propagandist of the unbridled act: anyhow, the
amusing type of fiasco mindset; he senselessly realistically
employs the senselessly realistic (dear Ravachol!). Another goes
straight to scribbling or making music hogwash, etc. etc. and
would like the sudation of his most embarrassing states be held in
awe as a type of foresight or even redemption. Forget it . . . !
Ultimately, another crosses the continent by train as, depending
what the situation calls for, a count or burglar, a profiteer or
diplomat, a gambler or marriage fraudster, a pimp or high civil
servant, for this multifarious activity alone satisfies his enormous
need for diversion (Manolescu, Charles de Hoffmann, *je vous
salue!*). If he happens to have *prodigious* talent, he becomes a
statesman and locks up thieves and guillotines murderers, because
half-measures won't do when dealing with the entirety of this
swindle en masse. Yet once he has power, he quickly elevates it to
an axiom and, after several minutes, even believes, since everything is always in flux, he is exercising it under the pretext that

the acts of violence he committed to escape boredom should now be punished. He installs former colleagues, whom he now sees without employ, profiteering, in embassy posts far and wide; taps (courage) — an artist and shoves him into school primers, where he does in fact belong, but where all tender idiotic good (yoo-hoo!) — poetry (bad poetry is always better) isn't as prominent, even though the whole thing now has a purpose after all, and thoroughly prepares minds for boring hypocritical positivism by patting the Church on the shoulder when it distorts Jesus, who otherwise would be too pernicious as an arch-Jesuit, into the catechism (rowing club) . . . And see: stench enters into the world and grows increasingly robust. The obvious (the lovely non-obvious) ceases to be so. The non-obvious (the instigated non-obvious) becomes a duty. (This: the aggregate of all impudence that this rogue has purloined — *trucs!*) But the intractable specter of boredom looms large and pale behind it all and ultimately seizes the whole gang in an abrupt grip: The statesman rings, the curtain rises . . .

17. War! *C'est la guerre!* Walk right in, gentlemen! Simply walk right in! . . . People run around chaotically, confused, frightened, horrified. Is there an end to it? A point? A purpose? Any sense? . . . These dear folk don't even know why they even exist, nor what was and what will be, and even the most subaltern deliberation that they are serving the private machinations of supreme individual swindlers will change little in their thinking; nor will the knowledge that those directing their battlefield deaths are staging this drama solely because they, too, are bored. The majority then begin to shoot not because they don't see through this hoo-ha, but because they take it as a (hoho!) sensation . . . After all, the

arrangement is good. The newspapers shout hurrah and telephone the ministries about motivational phraseology. The brass
band totters up and drowns out any alteration. Fantastic speeches
are conceived, polished to be of historical value, and dribbled out
to the already inebriated masses, high office in the offing, and the
dear Lord himself personally charged to patronize the slaughter.
And hot on the heels of this wonderfully crafted advertisement,
the first grenades explode. The gentleman up in his loge has his
spectacle, the populace a bloody way to pass the time, and dapper
Death, the only one who truly benefits from this venture, curtsies
from the boredom that inevitably overtakes both the audience
and actors once the first act has concluded . . . But look: They are
in the process (oh, oh, oh) of becoming ri-ra-republicans, so that
they may slave away for industrialists and other rastas. Yet if they,
too, saw through all this and finally gained full control over
themselves, they would face a choice between the most hideous
boredom, or . . . (I am imagining the yellow guard of the final
fury . . .)

18. The ever so popular distinction between culture and civiliza-
tion fractures in this fine perspective on how outsized the need to
numb yourself (to warble) . . . oh, with so-called intellectual stim-
ulation! Nothing more than an unbridled escalation of an excess
of boredom that has led many to delude themselves that they're
not bored at all. The reality is, however, in these moments you're
bored to the point of convulsion. In my view, it is highly probable
that all (*on m'excuse*) geniuses in the history of the world were
well aware of this, yet prudently kept their mouths shut. None
have yet bothered to reject this odious mental reservation. Clearly
the reason is as plausible as it is pathetic: No coachman would

admire anyone who gainsays the greatness of his thoughts by confessing they are no more than convulsive states. But if not for this foolish masturbation of vanity those suspenders would have had to hold up so unbearably long that . . . ? Presumably they deemed years of Madame's huffing and puffing en face more necessary than any honest excess downward before themselves (where the fit, believe me, is more tight than anywhere else) . . . What a primitive scam! They all died with reservations about their greatness (pah, devil!) arrayed on lips bearing last words. Even Voltaire and Montaigne. Pah, devil! . . . (One need not have read either Kant or Nietzsche: a single line is enough to induce vomiting . . .)

19. No, it is *not* likely. These whiners have conceded *nothing*. If you *truly* have, even just *once,* given this awful desolation surrounding you (spare me!) serious thought, this endless boredom that emerges from it, then you *cannot* help it: convulsions are unleashed and — you rage around yourself, at yourself . . .

20. I do praise the Asian. He lives for nothing, nothing at all, at most for his dolce f. n., which is merely a simple expression of the joyous intention not to notice oneself. A sublime layabout! (The European lives at times for a Tusculum, where all sorts of fantastic, that is, entirely boring, things happen). Thus the Asian also has no ac-an-art and isn't a soigné robber ltd., who quotes the classics in business correspondence (a belief pusher). In a little café in Geneva I once saw a gent from India sit immobile for an entire afternoon staring straight ahead. It was as if he were sleeping with his eyes open (good, good) . . . How disgusting it is to witness the crumpled ambition of our domestic porters of the spirit, being good Europeans. Cosmopolicretin! Culticretin!

21. Please, spare us, please, no feigned batting of eyelashes! No ardent biting of lips. Every kind of enthusiasm is precarious: the embarrassing admission that you can't do any better and *also* don't know any better. Thus the coherent rationale (and the incoherent, which is also coherent) brings no encouragement to finely attuned ears . . . Of the many paths that lead nowhere, the most pleasant are still those where retch-inducing ideas are so freely strewn about they arouse a particular curiosity. You stagger to them, exchange your otherwise indifferent thoughts for them, and discover, albeit no metaphysical torpedoes, well indeed — lovely thighs . . . feces, hardened feces in your noses, you bracket-twerps! . . . (Understandably, I hope these intellectual turds squatting on those miserable underbellies will hear it. Without a public, even the most well-conceived curse will fail to bring even one scrap of pleasure . . .)

22. Thighs are fantastic. Wars the most severe diarrhea. Freedom is an amusement park. Peace, *the* catastrophe.

III

23. Typical trait of all bourgeois riffraff: remove the danger from others that threatens their self-assurance, its greatness by the fact that it is — doubted. The short version: whoever is proud, arrogant, rude, he is . . . (sc.: openly self-assured). The long version: whoever is modest, shy, humble, he is (sc.: secretly self-assured!) . . . Sweet, sweet Mi! . . . In both cases: They are always opposed to self-assurance since this is the only way they might indulge the groundlessness of this quality in themselves as an asset. The ox is suspicious of such ends. The ox! Did he really know how to sweetly suspect: didn't his balls have to grow back? (They did!) . . . *Naturellement:* there is no such thing as self-assurance. The reality: having none. The tragedy par excellence (*oh là là*): — the grotesque . . . Oh, if I could, just once, for three quarters of an hour, handle things like a Saxon! Out of gratitude I wanted to become (now and then) a psychologist and feed vulturously with Geyers . . . In short: one ultimately needn't bring any glassy views into history. Into the he- ho- hu- ha- (aha) hysteria, however, there still may be some factually warranted capabilities that continually need to be spewed out (the swig around the axis).

24. Sweet, sweet Mi! You once rhapsodized (robe of black barège) between Evening Glory Fizz, me, and (alreeeady) four in the afternoon thus: "Bah already all kinds of jerking, bah one is polite, hands over money, or otherwise rewards the boy, whoopsydaisy the bird becomes arrogant, and rightly so if he takes every one that shows him respect for an absolute idiot, bah, is one, on the other hand, thus — reticent, stingy with praise (nice, *n'est*

pas?), or even just indulgent, with the same result in ultramarine, this time, however, because the boy considers *me* arrogant, whereas for me, as you know full well, you scoundrel, only the Fizz is truly important, and sometimes your incredible shoulder position etc., oh well, bah, but I have happened right upon an angelic little ploy, successfully oriental, and absolutely the best currently available in this area, I'm actually saying exactly the same thing to everyone that I *just* said to you, and that I'm *also* going to say to everyone from this point forward, and *that* too and that too, *that too,* that too, that too, nonsense . . . and nearly everyone, though always somewhat shaken, becomes usable and rather banknote-nice, please . . ." Sweet, sweet Mi! *Elle a un savon à la place du coeur* . . . the apocalyptic whore . . . *je me tais* . . .

25. you can gawk so blankly ahead that victory seems assured. Oh, it is difficult. About the scale: Mistrust jumps on hate, hate on mistrust, until you can't take it anymore and talk yourself into loving one another. The last psychic belly upswing of the (certainly, certainly) — blackout. If you gawk, however . . . you will have to constantly work with a crimp in your gaze (or in your voice). Assuming it would be technically possible to accomplish, it would ultimately lead to verbal injury (or injurious internal secretions). Oh, it is difficult . . . (Theoretically, the global man has long been banned — that he still practically grazes is just as inexplicable as the ban itself.)

26. One day at the Cottbus Cemetery as I observed that sorrow is merely the painfully intense attempt to conceal that you have none, I resolved:

    1. to henceforth write only postcards,
    2. to exact a fee for all services applied to me with a slap,

3. to humiliate myself (as so exquisitely rendered in the song) as often as possible,

4. to otherwise constantly wear the freshest clothes, to excel, and

5. to ask no single question (since any is inevitably silly) and to give no single answer (since any is simply demented) ever again.

Consequently, I nearly married. Yet at the very last moment I managed to forget a postcard. Thus, Point 1 should now read:

1. never again to assert having only written postcards.

This, then, is the secret of my so often admired self-assurance when dealing with waiters, widows, and business advisors.

27. Have you ever seen a drowned corpse? No? Then make sure to timidly keep your distance. Your vis-à-viper, who, as you know, is not familiar with such things either, would begin to act decisively in a heartbeat . . . if you have never seen a drowned corpse. Well, timidity is (as any genuine state) unfortunately unbearable and cannot be cashed in. The fellow who has to constantly look at such a corpse soon starts to fiddle with his fingernails so intently that he begins to have serious reservations about his manicure, and no longer able to endure this apex (ach!) — of self-indulgence he then all at once flips out: . . . a fatuous impudence, an outrageous gesture, a chic accent blaze up from the most tranquil ambience of coffeehouse or pub. And if a similar fit of fatuity fails to quickly blaze from your eyes, the entire affair is turned on its head: now *you* consider yourself absolutely decisive *because* you still have never seen a drowned corpse . . . As both sides of the brain steadily ramp up, a long, utterly idiotic rasping could be predicted . . . Thus: learn to master the high idiom!

28. The last disappointment? When the illusion that you're free of illusion reveals itself to be illusory. (The most bombastic maneuver of vanity: making yourself more stupid and wicked than you would care to be only to indulge the vanity that you're not vain. Horrible failure.) . . . The peak of naiveté? When someone at one stroke wants to learn the (ogodogodo) — truth. (Yet a slap in the face is ultimately just a desperate attempt to approximate. Phony tears, too, often seem more genuine than — the phony.) . . . Two jocular conundrums? Not really. Two bracelets.

29. An excellent cigarette is an absolutely necessity . . . All symptoms of a bad conscience (bing!), of guilt (bang!), like a deep blush, paling, stammering, unsteady gaze, compulsion to speak of that which betrays, etc. and other such nonsense, comes to the fore when sensitivity (lacking mastery of the higher idiom) reaches quite a high level, solely on the basis of this sensitivity, which so quickly anticipates these symptoms as instantly recognized possibilities that it is de facto no longer able to repel them (or actually even wants to: *the* condition . . .) . . . Such interminable sentence structures, so casually spewed after considerable psychological bankruptcy! ("My dear, your knee, please!")

30. Almost anyone who is very agreeable when silent arouses revulsion when deciding to speak. There's nothing I've done more frequently in (especially: good) society than chant a paean to all manner of riffraff. (Largely to attract attention: the aforementioned revulsion is very quickly drowned in a blissful surge of vanity.) . . . Moreover: consorting with citizens of the State is just a pointless exercise. Every rapprochement is in and of itself a humiliation (excl. vitalust), every fellowship, ditto. Its essence: eavesdrop on (pst! pst!) the erudite and inveigle their misgivings

from them. Oh, what would a grand hotel lobby be without reverberating misgivings! Appalling! What would a misgiving be without its reverberating! An idée fixe. Fixed (an amusing case) in vain . . . (fixed, fixed). Whoever still doesn't understand Gaia Afrania, who showed her ass to the praetor in the forum, doesn't yet understand the . . . oh, all right then: the swig around the axis!

31. *It's a long way to Tipperary.* No doubt. For upon closer inspection: psychology is a handicap. Every rule has its exception, without question. That is, as a rule. So be extremely careful: every rule should be made an exception, for the rule is the exception. (An important rule!) . . . There are only relative assessments of relative connections. And not even these exist. Psychiatrists and examining magistrates are, at root, the empty shells of ushers (traveling circus), since every (ooh la la) — psychological judgment is a task commissioned by the one being judged, the verdicts of which thus rarely elicit a favorable response because the one being judged, in self-ignorance, has erroneously formulated the request. The best judgments are demonstrably those that have been derived from the worst formulations, and the worst from the best formulations. (Small seedless fruits are the sweetest. Oh, those dear, indolent mugs!) Proven: the tremendous variety of judgments about (ha!) — bad people. (Those about good folk are always correct.) Secondary proof: judgments only interest juveniles when they hear them, but those high-born boys before anything has even been (stay!) submitted . . . Every piece of advice is outright lethal; but just en passant: pronouncing bad judgments about yourself is still the most sincere way to steer clear of the good ones, which are also false. *Tant de bruit pour une — occasion perdue?* . . . Sometimes, though, absolutely nothing helps: either grinning for

or against. They trust you all the same. Ah, where is the audience for *truly* tough guys? I've become so narrow and spratty . . .

32. Pos- possibilities of interaction. Man and woman (lady): best case, coitus; suboptimal case, something akin to copulation; worst case, erotic hocus-pocus (a conversation piece!) to which the adjective "pausal" (feeble, or: see the penal code) has to be applied. Man (gentleman) and man: best case, one appraises the curve of the lips of the fellow opposite and is silently (or, high-idiomatically) languid past the cheeks; suboptimal case, a faint-hearted tussle ensues, according to which dubious pastime each who is well versed lets the shoulders sag and victory or defeat and yourself and the other and everything are rejected and, in short, all's good (not good!); worst case, you crease your brow and on the whole display weighty matters, and with the proper form, in short, you prattle away (oh dear Sotades!) The swig around the axis! In the French province of Haute-Garonne on the Spanish border, the fabrication of freaks is still to this day the local indus-try (one deformed for 50 to 60 francs). This type of business would disappear in a flash if as a result of the aforementioned worst cases, which unfortunately predominate, the institution of compassion had never been established . . . *"But the genuine crip-ple?"* Well, you would be interested, if you'd already quite . . . again for Hegel, pacifism, and the eventual destruction of deformed babies . . . *I* prefer ladies!!!

33. There are days when everyone puts on a stupid face. And nights when the dumbest fellow still looks too important. And there are weeks and months and years and . . . the most flatulent words, the most lax pauses, the extended tongue, the long nose, et al., are thus tricks for more easily facilitating contact; all the more

in that each situation is untenable in every respect. You should let these lovely gestures take on a delicate tinge of madness (*this* is the high idiom!) and you will be amazed how excellently everything develops . . . And since merely impassioned (as it were) jabbering can shatter *all* interpersonal relationships (they are *always* constructs!) it serves as a healthy palliative as well. Apropos: as we know, people live together (until you . . .) in a web mostly of their own making and often very delicately spun (conjugal paranoia; Juan Suvarin and his Narva); alone in one even more delicate (until you . . .) . . . You should finally begin to stand up to yourself! You should begin!! You . . . !!! (I've been spitting on my own head in the quiet hours for some time already . . . Ah, I could give a hoot . . . — . . . Well, about what . . . ?)

34. Ladies are senselessly preferred. Every rule is an exception. Psychology a handicap. The swig around the axis: To hell with it all.

IV

35. Cartesius and Swift, notoriously, loved squinting. *Chapeau bas!* (Still . . .)

36. The greatest certainty in all matters is projected by whoever is convinced of the restless uncertainty of everyone else and is therefore sick of it all. The broadest awareness (Patent Oil Urinoir) is merely the ultimate uncertainty that the penultimate foists as certainty. The ultimate certainty is, as such, absolutely relished: *true* certainty (intense verve). Therefore, everything is utter pretense, since everything is uncertain (rastaquouèresque). On top of that: who hasn't felt when crying, as if lying, when smiling, as if dissembling, and when forgetting about his own face, as if betraying himself, eh? All mimicry (minor muddle): pretense . . . Camels believe in their masks. Those who observe them discover they're already playacting by simply opening their mouths. Keep in mind: you playact best when holding your tongue *and* facial expression (major muddle) . . . Naturalness (schuk schuk pra pra) unfortunately falls into the sweet realm of the unconscious: nevertheless, it has become a criterion for being a headmaster who elevates praise to a virtue, which is, of course, only natural; yet otherwise: a young son is considered natural today if he doesn't notice that his creator is a camel . . . Clapperboard: inevitably the so-called certain becomes uncertain if pretense turns against them; if the pretense becomes what speaks for the other, it is not what speaks against the other and often enough also against what now speaks for the other (*shut up!*). Since there is neither pretense nor certainty, the only remaining effective means is not to become

uncertain: not even wish to be certain at all . . . Thumb on shoulder, lock in on the position of the left nipple (roughly) of the person opposite, the bridge of the nose or the shoulder area, and do not yield. Under no circumstances. That's enough.

37. Seriousness can be so vigorously asserted that the victim (nonneigher) is unable to perceive how the fool opposite has already been mentally rubbing his hands gently for quite some time. The need to leap out of his present state (agoraphobia + word-rage) and into his correct state (his johnson, so to speak) is at its most moist right at this moment. This proves quite nicely how (hmm) — you could arrive at yourself via the back door if no heavy raids of your hinterland have succeeded, yet. For initially, every flâneur overestimates himself, and a keener fellow (verve) considers himself a *true* genius as long as it hasn't dawned on him that this is nothing more than the talent to become famous. At which point he quickly becomes debauched (*raté*), limiting his brilliant ability to create fructified trite platitudes out of allusions (talent) to his private affairs (Central 1098), and, if unlucky, he becomes famous anyway and fills his leisure time neighing in front of a hand mirror . . . (*Un oeil dit merde à l'autre.*)

38. Hey, what's all this about a demon? . . . Easy now . . . In fact, the distrust of the wild man in himself turns into a constant checking of his sentences, and ultimately he's certain he's able to decide to do anything he wants. All he has to do is make up his mind. And then the guy's demonic. As far as the wild woman is concerned, well — it's even more skewed than that: at first delighted and wonderstruck from indulging the gifts of her body, soon after exhilaration at its enormous (ecstastic) — high tension (flexing whip-like between head and toes . . . jubilant!)

and in the end the unbridled determination to try *everything* . . .
And just like that the gal's demonic. (Note to those slow on the
uptake: Everyone affects a kind of coquettishness in everything
they do; thus not every act of the will immediately produces hol-
low amazement. As for the demonic, there's no real reason to
believe in its existence.)

39. ever since I've become somewhat more aware of the existence
of graphologists, I have come to regain a modicum of trust in
bridge railings . . . A letter's effect on the minor muddle: puerile,
ridiculous; and on the major: idiotic, scurrilous. Handwriting
(quite honorable) is the most irrelevant piece of information an
oddball can reveal about himself. (And since there are no relevant
ones, well . . . there!) . . . With the primitive conclusions (Barbara)
it engenders, nothing is achieved (everything *solely* barbaric!): a
child's handwriting the most dangerous of all. And as far as
phased conclusions go (viennaworkshops phantasmagoria): your
own flattering suggestion leads you astray. Right into a detour.
Every (eh!) — scrap of handwriting is, for whomever it speaks, a
successful mystification . . . In the end, you always fall for it.
Always. Fall. For it.

40. And there are still (krrr!) — throats for which the not exactly
worst opinion from the neighboring throat is good enough.
Bunglers! I always have the worst, and loudly, though actually I
have none at all. Thus everything blooms from my throat . . . Each
one blusteringly vacuous! Every single one! Why always shove an
opinion into something, you drunken swine? Clearly: chame-
leons (brokerquills) are the dingiest back stairwells; however:
be empty, then, as empty as you are! After all, this is far more
pleasant: everything gets easier, looser, especially the gentleman

himself . . . For those who don't know it yet: the more easygoing, the looser he is, the more genuine he is; since he has no set plans in mind, it's easy to fill him up. Yet then again, you rogues, the minute is fast approaching (at the very least) when his hips will bend. The sidesplitting power of this Tibetan laughter: put-ons, cliquish types, glueboilers, all you know-it-alls, your skin's bursting. Look, it's inflated . . . Thus everything has been blooming from my throat for quite some time!

41. *"I see through you!"* — From this moment my distrust waned: the lad bored me . . . Ah, what a fine deed it is for some who have already forgotten how to menacingly conduct slick conversations for them alone, a poorly weeded puffball! (Moreover, if he's mollycoddling his patent leather shoes.) Is it any solace to know that useless members of human society still exist? No. In spite of it all. For they, too, occasionally look around, wet with pleasure. They, too, live so deeply ensconced between buttersoft eroticism and brainmush that even a shrewd demoness every now and then loses her cool in the face of their conduct. (This is *the* crime!) Oh, and how invigorating a miscue! Therefore, the puffball may be treasured and all conduct nurtured and flustered until this contrivance, born of delightful circumstance, is no more, can no longer be flustered. Nevertheless, you should keep in mind what Napoleon uttered when someone gave him his Egyptian Proclamation to read over (*"It's a bit gimmicky!"* — the actual words of this most excellent man), not perhaps as spiritual refuge, since only when you have managed to hold a conversation with your own prostate will you have some idea of your bearings. Up until that point, the sole, truly dignified human position is to lie *in effigie,* yet while keeping weight on the most risible body part,

and thus coming across as much more appalling opposite the starry firmament.

42. is an innuendo (definitionally considered), an insidiously fobbed off assumption that makes you perfidiously (yet often uselessly) defenseless; unless . . . If you don't react to it, you're taken for an idiot, or it's confirmed just by the fact that you've ignored it; if you do react to it, you're still taken for an idiot, because it's confirmed by your reacting to it, or for that very reason you're told with a smile that no innuendo was even made, rather what you heard was just the whistling of the wind. Unless you immediately accuse the one making the innuendo of having an improper relationship with a warmed-over filet mignon. A fabulous success.

43. *"A-a-a-and love?"* The sentimental man (mustashell) makes a swan of a goose. (That is love). And this because he really only senses *himself* the most clearly. The other (the contemplative) receives (didnyaseeit) — thoughts and ascribes them to his Ida . . . Eroticism? Ersatz sexuality. Instinct burns, knees are cold. The brain takes pity and prepares diversions for frayed nerves. Theater of the best kind . . . Those porters of the spirit currently rampaging around Central Europe, with style-trumpets blaring, emitting ominous notes that you should be done with eroticism by the age of thirty. What's left? Shpirit, eh? Scoundrels! But just have a look at their women! . . . Mimicry . . . Even those with radiant mien only achieve it by mustering that peculiar patience to their unwavering efforts to draw from it (hop to it!) — profundity. Although every woman makes fun of the type (mimicker) she's gotten hitched to anyhow, she, too, whose radiant mien lands her in bed, is not occasionally above disgraceful conduct

herself: *"It's completely irrelevant anyhow, how often a man . . ."* (Madame blushes!) *". . . my husband says that too, sure."* Actually, *he* is the only one who does say that, *ma pauvre*; for no woman says what she's thinking, but rather only what strikes her, and she gets that from her husband (eh?) . . . How easy it is indeed to (hmm) — convince her that sexuality is the only certainty! And how difficult to make her despise it! That this still happens, even today: These little men need to drum up a drop of spirit to pass the time (which is nothing but desperation!) . . . Hardly anything is more amusing than this blathering (style-trumpets) that is supposed to make Leo more desirable to Madame. But it only works so-so. It's no better than sleeping with a pseudo-intellectual.

44. Objectivity in the ribs! *Very* objective! . . . The observation of that huge, ancient knight's armor; fellows such as Casanova and Henri IV knew how to cope so well with their lues: take a stroll through European cities and you'll see knights of this (pardon?) — sad sort . . . It is at present, in every respect, quite advisable to die off. Folks these days no longer know what they should do with *their* après (oh, those bleak pauses!). Once upon a time, there was no après, my gentlemen poets. (Indians are still spirochaetan-virulent today, yet healthy!) Oh, if only these old instincts were still with us, yet the vitalities that go along with them have long since vanished! They were once perpetually busy; no one had any time to get bored (to trumpet): They inhaled right to the depths of their lungs, copulated, hunted, ate voraciously, brawled, boozed, copulated, swam, grunted, copulated, slept, and the day was at its lovely end. Now instincts have only fourteen hours free instead of twenty-four that serve (quiet!) — professional life or (pfff!) — contemplation, which has the sunny task of smoothly

cajoling a gentleman right out of his instincts, so much so that while he might actually believe he's really an amazing fellow, he's astute enough to take a back seat. Apes! Degenerate apes!! Miserable apes!!!

45. *"What do angels do when they sing not?"* Dear Jakob Böhme, surely they moan that they are not . . . (No one lower than that lamebrain Dante . . .)

46. Well then, the middle deck would like to know what they should do with their (still quite intact) health. Since it's only noticed when so much of it has been lost, this trickster's suggestion is well worth considering: "Give up at once!" (Capisce?) Imposing! . . . Not a chance! Frigidity is only a very low-level (well) — *béguin.* An absolutely frigid person is — dead. Flat out dead. Yet you always end up disappointed in yourself, as if taking a coatrack and standing it in the same place. At twenty you've got to jettison the monocle, at thirty get rid of the cigarette behind the ear and realize once and for all that the only way you can be rid of Madame is by suddenly beginning to — love her (if a more complicated situation, become jealous . . .).

47. At the bitter end . . . you become malicious, purely out of boredom. Then you become bored of being malicious. And ultimately, you begin collecting little chocolate pictures. Idealism is still criminal realism. A *bocher* who remains gentle is somewhat less creepy (since he's an idealist) than an Imaginist gone wild (since a realist). Who might've been the very one responsible for inventing the ampule "soul"! Perhaps the somewhat disappointing sight of the naked . . . This disappointment, however: you should yank yourself by the ear, screw up your courage and admit, since

opportunities no longer bring what others used to get from danger — you have a secret admiration for your own legs . . . Yes, you take it so far as to *almost* entirely feign your tabula rasta in order to strike the most shattering blow with this seemingly scant remnant of the "almost," which naturally strikes your own flesh: . . . one last little pleasure . . . one last little rage.

48. Venusgazes are the only certainty. The demonic is a piece of filet mignon. Bedspirit-trumpeting is barbaric. The soul is no bridge railing. Love, swanshit.

V

49. The scantiest detail always impugns the overall impression. If one knows Chinatown or Tiffany (bijouterie), then that quiet vacancy of the senses rises again soon enough, for which toast with jam provides no solution. And since every declaration is much less important than you think, when any take you in it's preferable to indulge only in the wispiest syntactical steam. Impulsiveness is *no* argument. And experts who from the very outset speak so loudly that all those with fire insurance are of the same mind, they have within them . . . knockout. Madame's breasts bounced. Mr. N. with a mattress on his chin (mattresses are hard to pluck) convinced himself that a bad conscience is quite variable. Even the wispiest of the wispy can only really dispute the sound (little sound). You strive over and over in vain to find just the right word. ("Perlimpimpim," said Mr. N., affectedly.) . . . Gingerly up and down you go, clutch your old noggin, and at this moment an idea might suggest itself and is elevated to a principle: *le comble du grand écart . . .*

50. In that desperate lethargy (half desperado, half fatalist) that's decisively disposed toward nothing, thus toward everything, tension squats for a double-dosed falsetto. When heard, it's as if you were ultimately being stripped of all patience. I overheard the jockey Rudi Etvöes say to the lady who meant extra income for him: *"If I want to be good, I always have the rotten luck that I end up wanting to screw the other guy over."* — *"Not me."* — *"Sorry?"* — *"Je m'en fous!"* . . . The falsetto. Double-dosed. (When will the day come when folks are allowed to have their armpit

hair stroked for dessert, in the Aero-Palace, 3000m above Nice, eh?)

51. Perlimpimpim... Every apartment you enter for the first time is in order (well) — sarcastically; partly: ... because you are constantly aware that the joy (beefsteak) or polite demeanor (breakfast) with which you are greeted has been preceded by seconds of sheer annoyance, or even hatred; and because, on the other hand, a kind of duress creeping into the face of every person who enters the room can be detected right when they're on the threshold: you have the impression that everything they say will be deceptive, that while still on the stairs they were already happily sneering in anticipation, that your annoyance or feeling of hatred directed at them for that very reason cannot have escaped their notice ... partly: ... *déganter*: why not openly admit that the onion has been peeled? Or: why not talk (warble on) about Mama's Little Bayram, or about the soupy talion, which Passoskskaya exacted with stolen *papillotes*, or about the *gasconnade* of the court tailor Simeon Achselschweiss ... partly: ... because every apartment has to be just such a *tripot* with forbearance of surcharges. Perlimpimpim ...

52. Phlogistic *crapule*: wanting to have no system is the same as a new one. Truth (*la blague*) *cannot* even become a problem if it must be a linguistically acceptable premise. Every person has always believed in much too much: you don't have to buy into *anything at all*. This type of malice (no system) is just the disguised trepidation at your own fecklessness (not even: senselessness!) ... I am digressing into sheer babble: the thought alone could become a problem, most acutely where it falls between the poles of true and false that it depends on the tiniest nuances. It is

here, however, that the private individual is cognizant that one cannot decide apodictically but only (heh, heh) — suss out to which of the two poles the thought *seems* to be moving closer. And this way of thinking is at once problematic. (May plausibility remain the only criteria. Merci!) . . . You *cannot* let yourself buy into anything! If I say: "I deny the truth," I am standing between the poles of true and false since I'm asserting that truth does not exist: thus I want *this* proposition to be true. A perfect contradiction: the content of the proposition is refuted by the proposition itself. Every proposition is therefore false because it denies the possibility that something could be true . . . At this point things begin to nicely shimmer. You belch. And everything yellows, somehow . . . You're always mistaken. Always. Everyone. Always. Everyone. Always everyone . . . (Compulsive actions? Or: uncontrollable rage? Or . . . ?)

53. Or: raisins. Starting tomorrow you simply need to resolve to say instead of belly, riffraff, instead of index finger, Semp: — and things will brighten right up. At the moment I really appreciate the word "raisins." When I utter it, I think of a mix of midwives, MPs, and cottage cheese . . . (*Memento laeli:* the more improbable an occurrence, the more it is probable. I contend that I am an occurrence no more probable by the improbability of this assertion. And thus prefer to occur without assertions.)

54. A fairy tale (genesis) . . . naiveté originally perfected. Loss of naiveté (why?) and of the senses (naiveté?). Subsequently, the quandary: busyness. Initially: the unawareness, thus dull desperation (bored). Later: awareness, thus great desperation (enormously bored). Therefore: new needs, for which you toil and leave others to toil. Thus: commerce: wheeling and dealing. Further: new

needs, new deals. And since the boredom continues to grow, you begin to theologize and philosophize and in the end begin to make money *from it* . . . Diagnosis: chronic agony. Remedy: naiveté? O sweet naiveté! . . . A genesis? Well, no. Solid stupidity!!! Not tempered by plausibility. A fairy tale (such as Poe's *Eureka* or Weininger's *Sex and Charac.*) . . . You still might cobble together (chirp) an amusing alternative, something along the lines of:

1. Either: switching off consciousness (fakir, haoma).
2. Or: conscious schism (the head waiter).

    ad 1. Construction of the nonhuman (the goggle-eye).

    ad 2. Construction of the subhuman (the scatterbrained).

Both constructions are derived from the same source: — (insert your preferred noun, if you please! Something like: mosquito-bureau!!!).

    ad 1. Rearmost senselessness (Nirvana brand).

    ad 2. Foremost senselessness (tariff trends in the passementerie trade).

I'll pass! . . .

55. In any case, morality is the least expedient means for handling any sort of business. In the sense that because one is able to maintain a good business (morals) as opposed to a far better one (no morals) (what delightful transparency!), it's quite easy to admit you basically have no opinion, you appear to be — more or less — unleashed and have needlessly dragged around a concocted idea of the worst kind . . . The elimination of morality might therefore be achieved through the introduction of brokers in marital matters. Or by impeding the enjoyment of compote. Or simply by baths.

56. the joke is the only bearable type of repetition of long-ago exhausted inanities. Wherever things are serious, that is where frogs gather (the like-minded!). The more convulsively funny a guy is (an assy Rhum!), the more he steps in it (an assignment, renown) . . . A joke? Leading oneself ad absurdum (to a *chignole*): à la galette . . . (Charlot Chaplin: Gerhart Hauptmann — an orphan) . . . And humor? I say nothing more than: Kempinski (or: the rear door left ajar for limp drunk sortments-sentiments) . . . Oh, there's a kind of lurching screwball joke you let be on you, for your own pleasure, so as to be pillaged for a few months by a feminine torso (well then) that spreads into utterances causing blood to accumulate in the calves of others (so to speak). Of course all of this just pisses me off. Really pisses me off. (The milk of outmoded ways of thinking under the fl-flash of the most dazzling blood!) . . . But this, too, is merely pleasant, not comprehensible at all.

57. Being unsuccessful is basically a given. Success? A masterly mistake, more or less. Nothing's correct. (Not even this.) The more vehemently order is proposed, the more rapidly disorder ensues, ultimately displacing it. If someone were able to provide *the* idea (the latter: sense), everything would have to be clear to everyone and everything would be in most excellent order. Supposedly. But, this . . . all ideas are (etc. and similar nonsense) flat out mishaps. An idea? A success. Therefore: mishap. Christianity, for example, an ingenious protean occurrence that has endured as good business (morality), that has the Great War, which was bad business (with *and* without morality), on its conscience: — paranoia having the nature of the most vehement desire, driven onward from the lack of caned headmasters, incest, easy ways out,

and expansive self-love . . . (*"Love your neighbor as . . ."* etc. and similar nonsense) . . . Heh, how's that self-love working out? Thus: sometimes you love your self-hatred (so as not to grow deformed), but ever again self-hatred and despair (mascotte bar). This is not self-love but vanity, *naturellement*. If in fact there were such a thing as self-love, one could rightly be quite vain about it, yet for that very reason wouldn't be in the end, because self-love is not vanity, but an animalistically gifted condition (use the pasture). As for your neighbor, if your love him as you would yourself, this solely serves your own vanity, and you shouldn't be so amazed that so much loving is going on . . . The difference between J. Christ and Ch. Huysmans (*"Do unto others what you don't want them to do unto you!"*): both were successful and therefore had no success at all . . . By the way, blows often incur the greatest degree of devotion, gifts the greatest trouble. You might be tempted to come up with ideas. Nevertheless, I've hit upon a rather practicable way out (I'm really flattering myself!): whatever I cannot accomplish on the telephone, I acquire by theft, and if that doesn't work, then I help myself by faking a brawl . . . (*Après moi, la blénnorragie!*)

58. Masterpieces (speak more quietly!) of world literature: such a *vertiginous con* you close your eyes (in youth), continue to spin, and ultimately (if wanting to avoid getting found out) are led to believe you've attained a viewpoint and can start working on yourself . . . Art!!! The most infantile form of magic. Spend a few weeks with the esoteric sciences and you will discover that occultists are just healthier babies. All art magazines (*Sturm*-blabber, *Aktion*-blather, *Fackel*-babble) are just *separate* supplements of the corresponding dailies (external feuilletons). *The Neue Wiener Journal,* the afternoon edition of the *B.Z.*, and the *Matin* are in

every respect much more credible and absolutely to be recommended. (They are so blatant about giving space to whomever has money, to each and every lie, to every Magog, and naively allow snoops to "extract" from books before they've even appeared, that it's such a joy.) . . . Each of the best books of world literature were written with the intention of being the greatest book of all time: psychologically the sole bearable prerequisite in those days for writing books. Today it can only be like this: the desire to create the impossibility for any book ever to be written again with that intent. If it happened to pan out this way, then: who would be left to write bad books? . . . The best book: the one never written (Napoleon, Rimbaud, Lautréamont, Schukoff) . . . I would be happy to hear that these pages are the *last* crap ever written. I would be very happy indeed.

59. (Napoleon? The greatest blagueur of all time. Rimbaud? Of all poets. Lautréamont? Of all blagueurs. Schukoff? A blague of *me*.)

60. Lust is the only vertiginous con that I hope will endure.

61. Obviously I really don't spend much time at all with the likes of myself. I no longer even hold out the hope, for what it's worth, of being introduced to myself. Oh, these beastly relationships, all of them! (I really do favor the Hotel du Roule in every town.) . . . On your own, you're never on the right path. It's not a certainty, either, that you're walking the straight and narrow. (Observations are being *made!*) You should finally start to make clausal leaps with your legs!!! I very much suspect that I'm just müllering. Really . . . ?

62. Lust is everything. Masterpieces are not using the pasture. Passion is talion. Jokes are incest. Morality is a broker.

VI

63. This utterly savage stench naturally is not a consequence of human acts of heroism alone, but of everything: senselessness surging out of senselessness. If East Africa is to be subjugated by the blood of heroes, if missionaries allow themselves to be thrashed, if philosophers starve to death, all this is as senseless as any life, such as my life, which is very determined not to suffer a hero's death, nor to have the least little mission, and certainly not any philosophy whatsoever . . . Fixatoir: (ictus on the etymon please!) — the do-gooder is hated by the victim of his benevolence (excessive altruism is demoralizing) just as the scoundrel (noble type) is for the horrible suffering he has inflicted. Both are simply performing the senseless. Lately: all four. It hardly raises an eyebrow that reprobates are by and large loved more ardently than choirboys (*la barbe!*), and they are only loved this way if they are truly good — at malice. (One is truly good *only* from malice!) Thus, tantrums never occur as frequently as where (hopsdodderoohhhhh!) someone loves someone else . . .

64. Every writer who wants to be considered important (i.e., *every single one!*) makes sure that a quarter of the excesses with which they augment their biography are not unimportant. One accepts that the situation is unbearable and lives off it (albeit not exactly in villas). Excessements should be treated like phlegm! Leaked bile!! Oh, you damned mirror!!! . . . If you perceive your own stench as fragrance, then at least spare everyone else from it. Beautiful women often cause even regular idiots to act moronically: it would thus be rather delightful to play the part of the

gifted fiend (with soft relative clausal leaps) and to bag all the hottest from below. Moreover, chuckling over one's own chuckling fails. And at once anger rears its head . . .

65. Deep down, you never truly have control over yourself. And how could you! (All clothes have grotesque effect.) Imagine: the silence of those present annoys you, and you begin speaking about it, which annoys you all the more, although . . . (onerous thoughts such as: "What do we care about neurosis theory!" or: "Is Odol mouthwash the best for the heart?") . . . After just a few short sentences we're beyond furious. Why? . . . The surest way to withstand silence: to also be silent. This purple experience, well . . . You can revel in your hatred of others if it goes unnoticed. The only way to maintain the veneer is by keeping your hate, your betraying and undermining, undetected . . . Voilà: rage decides to exact its revenge. The gentleman frenetically runs riot, *very* frenetically . . . However: oh gallery of all feeble gesticulating — : for what? For what? Revenge for what? . . . Huh? . . . (Yet you'll never coax a fart from a corpse with that one. Perhaps, though, you'll get a line from Joachim Friedenthal, who's supposedly still alive.)

66. Briefly, it's enough to have convinced yourself that the most peculiar and refreshingly curious creatures are always foreigners, disliked for some obscure reason, who to their benefit are distinguished from the soapscum of their respective milieu by the fact that they do not unleash their will on their intellect (Bolsheviks). Truly, humans are neither capable of a universal trope (cash obligation) nor of eradicating poverty to enrich the world, nor of making social existence more bearable by lying less. (I am firmly convinced that I'm otherwise a polite person and am just killing time.) . . . You really no longer can believe in the swell of humanity

heralded by the Buddha (a typical borderline case of ichthyosis and paranoia) if you're forced to watch daily how what most gets a rise out of the chicest street-corner heroines is when the wives of bank directors look down on them. It really is too much. I'm gazing at Monte Salvatore. I believe I can see the hairs of its mount from this street, so imaginatively named after it. And I tell myself: "Laissons la salade. Faisons un grand arrangement."

67. There exists a void of especially explosive impact. You go out (damn it all!) among people to feed your hatred of them, but . . . you smell this void and cannot go on (not even with your legs) . . . And you know what's up: all of it unstable self-stumbling of the most onerous kind, all of it an inability to maintain sangfroid (even silence doesn't help you here), all of it a racket ipsius generis twice over (wagon-like you pull your psyche across the land), all of it untenable, under all circumstances . . . You can't even hold onto the fact that you cannot hold onto anything, esteemed enemies . . . The gentleman frenetically runs riot: from — *void-rage* . . .

68. "And a man's life's no more than to say 'one.'" (Shakespeare m.p.) Well, I maintain that I can't even count to one. (A human life: having been delivered) . . . In dealing with people who immediately steer every conversation to heights where it clearly never belongs, it is recommended that you consider Goethe a subjugated Indian child. Among other things, it stimulates appetite. (My last wish would be: just once to be able to put one over on myself; or: just once to be able to really get the better of myself.)

69. The previous three lines have a triple meaning. Please mind the work, reader . . . (scoff like underwear . . .)

70. Using a linguistic formulation will not make a dismal condition (rheumatic fever, la purée, an abnormal growth) more bearable . . . At first, it often seems that multiple formulations might benefit a thought; but later it seems too much has been lost by this; and ultimately a single formulation is enough to make it utterly ridiculous. The thought process? Crossroads. You could continue for hours, *windblown* in all directions interminably . . . Latest offshoot: every thought is a tantrum (at least a little). Contrary to the brazen calm and safety of the environment, including the porters of the spirit. Yet this concentrated insight only makes you all the more furious. Is not rage the most senseless thing? . . . A minor observation on disposition: if you're in a mindless rage, you often have the feeling that (pepepe-pépère) at this moment life makes perfect sense. Rage, then, is life itself? Though certainly: the most sincerity is surely in rage; though certainly: all other conditions are bearable only because rage remains latent in them, or one dissimulates . . . Yet: senselessness, having reached its zenith, is rage, rage, rage and long devoid of any sense . . .

71. Not having any money is almost proof of the contrary. Having some, a catastrophe. (*Every* conviction a disgrace.)

72. After a good dinner, I am more firmly convinced that no idiot so often thinks himself to be idiotic as (well, yes) — the non-idiot. Yet in this lies the real difference. Pas la peine! Every sincere non-idiot is a cynic to boot. (Cynicism: an outright absence of one-sidedness!) From a cynic to someone running riot is, by the way, just a short — pas (la peine?). The foremost cynicism is so many-sided that it becomes one-sided. You naturally realize this and become enraged. And the insincere non-idiot: . . . this person

is *good*. Who doesn't feel like they're about to puke? . . . (Who is still not *well?*)

73. (Feeling!) . . . So, then: somewhat professorial! Half-listen: a feeling arises when the body senses something is happening (Yvonne) and is thinking about it. If successful, the feeling is happily eliminated and the thought turns to yourself alone. And it's here that every strong individual feels like puking. Who wants to get to the bottom of it? Since consciousness (Patent Oil Urinal) is always only able to deal with itself, always only able to prove itself to itself (declinations!), even when it wants to refute itself! To catch your own meaning — with *this* apparatus? And even *the* meaning! ("Qui est là? Yvonne?")

74. The private citizen is out of sorts . . . Consciousness is vanity: boredom incarnate. Hate: the feeling of unsatisfied vengeance for wounded vanity, thus a severe symptom of low self-esteem (as long as it's not some lackluster sport). For you hate when you speak, and not only who is listening, but also yourself. Since only vanity can induce you to speak, it is, however, already affronted by the very act of speaking. So this vengefulness continues to remain unsatisfied, as it can only be mollified by knowing how to fill the void. Subsequently: boredom of vanity, boredom of hatred, boredom of revenge, boredom of rage, boredom, boredom, boredom . . . The canal ring is closed. The private citizen farts.

75. One possibility would be, perhaps: to consciously let loose, to leave yourself open to captivation by the most cryptic, most hidden farces and subterfuges — as *the* great surrender, which represents the sole possibility for your unconditional self-withdrawal:

the kick — away from yourself. (Applied to the cosmos at just this opportunity!) . . . Charlatan! A most infantile rager!! You are there!!! . . . Sometimes I'm really amazed that *everyone* doesn't suddenly begin to fly into a rage, or at least stop everything they're doing . . . Cock-a-doodle-do!!! . . .

76. Ultimately, even the most idiotic babble is an opportunity. Behind every sentence you must unequivocally intimate wild laughter; likewise behind every muscle movement optical in nature; otherwise you become — a serious person . . . In sum: is not the human brain merely an inherited chronic abscess? On the other hand, there is the fact that if I did not have this abscess would this idea even have occurred to me, at all. *Everything* is a symptom. Language as well as its outcomes. It's no point of view not to have one. The Earth moves (somehow), and thought is likely no more than a symptom of this movement . . . Since we have no meaning (the void), we succumb to the delusion that we have meaning, or, the more agreeable case, to the delusion that we're not deluded. We are thus incurably demented . . . That this blissful state ought to have been the result of a millennia-old abscess is almost a reassuring thought. Thought? Epochal! Lunacy? Secular! Is that not also a delusion? O long hours, O long hours . . . Cock-a-doodle-do! . . . To be sure: yet it is the most tenuous, the last, the most *glaring* lunacy . . . Therefore, I can allow myself to shout with joy cock-a-doodle-do. (I just shouted cock-a-doodle-do . . .) . . . *Cock-a-doodle-do!!!* . . .

77. Very gentle narrative tone: if you overlook the fact that the game is played for money in this world, pay attention to the fact that some people already have it. Do you play just for the sake of

playing? Or, to play your aces? Or, to cheat? You should definitely be for collecting little chocolate pictures and presenting them back to the public when the number collected has exceeded 481. Or should you be against it? Yet being against is ultimately too much. Nothing but müllering? Actual müllering? Wouldn't this just be the same thing? You would have to lie down silently and breathe your last. Unfortunately, you cannot because you're making too much noise. Well, Jacques Lebaudy, Emperor of the Sahara, was a truly great man any way you slice it. Wait, wasn't Footit the Clown even greater? Or Pankhurst? But Sirius, that stupid star, is even greater. Who wants to be called "sewer grating" for a whole Sunday? Or who "Hämbo"? Or who "Womwa"? . . . L.T. . . . — ? — . . . (Last Things) . . .

78. *Grand Marnier! Ruban rouge!* (See next one down!)

79. Nonetheless the sow ennobles from the arid post office, why *de mortuis nil nisi bene,* ragged dogs, where nevertheless *nemo potest peccare ab umbilico et inferius,* in every respect the april-pregnant baldachin-pug should be left by the wayside, Earth a gigantic dilettantism that doesn't conquer life, on, on you knights of loosened lust, and geniuses worry about overwhelming, a caustic on ice cream, what a dessert, heavily homey and mushflowered veinousearthen rocketexpulsionpurposes, the young condemned and the man himself the most important paramour and most revered amen, belly thy symbol is called navel, navel thy name is Hecuba, hunchbacked virgins, to affix all his vanity, the bravest, again the driver urged the oxen onward and with his usual sluggishness into the great day of blessed recognition, lace-curtain-layabout Villon and Ulenspiegel too, the notorious crook and pimp, if they were alive today they would find no publisher tralala

but once dead it suddenly doesn't matter anymore, eh eh, can you come along? great the groundbreaking conductors' amazement, respecting yourself where do you begin, it should all generally be approved, ach gawd not that li'l Moritz i'se love-n-hate ya not me whacha know me, the raindrops all streamer'd he will know thanks to you, hope not, Porkopolis bursts a uniform, this plagiarizer of slit windows extirpated be praised, that one, though, those squalls oh dear, word-spewing magazine editors, quite delightful these sentences, skates gliding on the mons pubis, if it came to him speechwise, and the girls wheezing in swollen vestibules for everything, why doesn't anybody ask, oh eternally moist Julie, lust murder only among cannibals, and also people as ideas perpetually climbing over themselves peering into the world harmless vain powertwits and ultimately jackhammers, every minor will recognize it that day a bookseller fobs Mörike's work on them and see a cardboard display holding condoms, yes yes, have you a lovely derrière, if not, well then, and georgmüllering gently and impetuously, who doesn't think about gentle Joseph, vile the virtuous and angelic praise of Messrs. Papamalady, a joke to appreciate the juices of someone who's climaxed with such brilliant effort, deux yeux disent merde à moi je me couche de bonne heure, at da crib now youse again an' nuttin from da left, do you love Eveline she's a hard-working gal and does her husband, jazz king of the air, Offenbach, his meaning seems unmistakable like yes this is all nonsense from bullshit bones, but to open very sensibly in the street, take two fingers of rice and be a gypsy every three months, rare a Jewish councilman, a fine move and powders himself after shaving don't you think, bridgethunder tunneljoy, women a perfidious race in general, oh Ovid, oh information from Vöglein & Schenierer, brochure post-paid in the lavatory, an organ grinder isn't a broom, either, philandering men, gentlemen and degenerates, since indeed policemen at sail, the Rhine cruise remains on hold until a diktat forbids Philippe to flaoutter but it never will happen, not agitated by the gouty echo of puddlelickers and genderfingers, easily said in the event of non-payment you repeat it on the green meadow, whether or not it offers me hazy sweetness and is cool, as yep in paradisiacally expectorated lungs Javanese morning connoisseurs already in early adolescence indulging themselves pathologically, an excuse, he had it in him, only those in rude health have stupider things to do, unless every lady doesn't practice good hygiene, she wants to see the Pilatus and passionately rejects syphilis, quite stormy, kid, you can dance, changes her address, though, in spite of reports about cooliefever next to cagey pupil-nutcase and seer-fruitcake, lining up braggarts against the wall or so they believe, la ritirata manquée, *go on and take care of yourself,* you snotty brat, the demolishing of the paprikacothurn, metaphysical racketeers, all targeting and slashing and screaming when they hit the mark and all of it pointless mouseshit nothingness, hallo-dri-oh life-insurance-slit-hunger and have to have a say, an abomination, Oscar je vous salue, payable in deferred pondleg installments with halberded pelisses, youth and ink and egg, a german-somersault on springs, the goiter ends with bad luck, oh no how you cough with that collar where did you get it, and have not skedaddled out of love for the midlevel berrybuck, stupidities are performed like taking bathing trips I therefore beg so dearly for them, minister-exchange-heretic recurring variety of hardly brawny comrades, dimwits sunrays, ha thus he does not dream of esquadrilles pills, and of parlorpepper and beaucoup de beurre, and a blow to the chin, aha, that lends

the daisies and especially the Coupe Jacques Plombières astral
valor like only . . .

80. *Cherries Jubilee!* (Gargle slowly!) O brouhaha, brouhaha . . .
ha ha . . . ha ha . . . ha . . . ha . . .

81. Give the cosmos a kick! *Vive le rasta!!!*

Lugano, March 1918

THE LOOSENING SONG

As I sat once in the juvie kennel
chewing on a most rotten conundrum,
the hands of a terrible tyrant fell
and beat me good like a drum.

Now in my attire of evening dress,
as calm and loose as anyone could be,
and no lady has for me too much sass,
no tricks and cons ever to worry me.

Emblazoned in my head is the motto:
"Ye've never ever seen the likes of me!"
Yet the gesture follows the gait just so:
"All do know me oh so profoundly!"

(The rhyme and iambic form is for mnemonic-technical and therapeutical-suggestion purposes only.)

It is recommended to commit "The Loosening Song" to memory without delay and then, and only then, to change locale.

Repeat it quietly to yourself (it should be recited once daily before going to sleep and after waking in the morning) as you enter a dance hall, seek out a quiet corner, making sure that the couples dancing can be observed from that angle, order a Cointreau triple sec, and have the waiter tell the bandleader to play "Du kleine Klingelfee" (keeping every irony immobilized at arm's length) and "Emma, j't'ai connue au cinéma." Until the first note of one of these splendid songs is played, you should keep busy with determining the strength of purpose of this venture, the residual target of which (a lady) you may now pick out in the hall if no other has presented itself. As soon as the selection has been made (please, no approach just yet!) you should feel delighted and admit that you are, over and above all of this, in such a state of mind that the designation "Last Loosening" is altogether appropriate, especially having read up to this point, yet it does not encompass that outright monstrous feeling of power emanating from the whole body and its wide-ranging brain.

You should indulge in this feeling of power for as long as it lasts in its undiminished fullness. As soon as it starts to wane, turn the page.

THE BELLY SONG

A clever fellow may well dare
to drop a word, and have it heard,
yet never leave your belly spare
should you call on a lovely bird.

PART II

THE HANDBOOK OF PRACTICES

PREPARATION

Prior to reading the lessons in the second part of this Handbook, you should advance order the following with an eye to having it served in a couple of hours:

Eggs Florentine (Cherry)
Crêpe à la Parisienne
Langouste sauce mayo
Pineapple with brandy
Petits fours (St. Marteaux carte blanche)

Once you have done so, begin reading, during which time you're not allowed to drink, only smoke. After each fragment, pause one minute, after each section, five minutes, yet do not look at the ceiling, only at the couples dancing, especially at the selected subject (or photo).

Should you suddenly feel unrestrained joy while reading, then either a very disagreeable shortcoming or a safer method has been discerned, which in the past might often have given you a reason for despondently not following through. Particularly effective fragments such as these should be underlined and reread three times. If a few of them refer to how you should conduct yourself with women, then even greater the joy from being in such close proximity to your test subjects. Give into it without letting undue reflection hinder you: the cerebral intoxication this reading produces could not be more intense.

1st Motto:	Be more than you are, be nothing! Then you shall be everything.
2nd Motto:	*T'en laisse pas conter!*
3rd Motto:	Every rule is an exception.
4th Motto:	*Vous pouvez bien m'aimer.* *Moi j' m'en fous,* *pourvu que j'vive.*
5th Motto:	Lov'ly lov'ly little Leenie you've got gams so fine and sheeny. If ya weren't jus' totally batshit, ya wouldn't be on your duff like a twit.
6th Motto:	Always keep yourself squeaky clean. Luck may come your way at any time.
7th Motto:	*Du culot, c'est beau. Mais du* *Serner, c'est — mehr!* *(La Rousse)*
8th Motto:	What's newest isn't always more important. Quite often the tried and true can be new.

I

ELEMENTARY MATTERS

1. In life, there are essentially no masters and no servants. All men are slaves to their own abilities and temperaments. If you always bear this in mind, you won't find it very difficult to guide your own conduct, and the conduct of others.

2. If things are not going well for you, make an effort to conceal the fact. On the other hand, if things are going well, hate and envy will appear around you, so act as if you have a lung or bladder ailment and purchase a cemetery plot. All animosity will fade.

3. As for the powerful, for whom your meager wealth is scarcely a concern, but rather just something to be taxed, simply feigning exhaustion should suffice. The exhausted are harmless.

4. Always act as if you take life seriously. Intelligent people, in the event that they actually believe it, will consider you trustworthy; if not, they will consider you intelligent.

5. As long as you still distrust yourself, you'll remain sentimental.

6. Positive feelings are nothing more than signs of weakness. The truly superior person (verve), no matter the vicissitudes of physical sensations, always evident to the connoisseur, displays a great indifference around his lips.

7. Nothing arouses suspicion more quickly than a non-bourgeois lifestyle without it being clear what advantage it brings. Spread the word that you're looking for a good auto dealer, and the whole world will open its arms to you.

8. In those hours of profound self-loathing, never completely avoidable as the indomitable longing for an inner foothold creeps over you when, above all, you're keenly aware of the fiasco of your own existence and agonizingly aware of the great nothingness we all face, do the following: drink two cups of hot chocolate, take an aspirin, and lie down in bed. (Hours such as these would be avoided if it were possible to avoid the predisposition for such an inner recurrence through poor sleep or overexertion.)

9. Again and again you encounter folks who prove that it really is rather easy to pass off a virtual cretin as a genius (well, OK) to anyone in the world. Yet don't let this fact lead you to the conclusion that great ability is synonymous with publicity. They are merely (distantly) related.

10. Avoid feeling special when you see someone else make foolish choices. A third person might notice and tap you on the shoulder at the next opportunity.

11. Devote some time to the works of ethicists. The more rigorously you do so, the more serenely will you come to appreciate your own polar opposites.

12. Never fan your own flames. You run the risk of being taken for a delicate, innocent virgin or, compared to Gilles de Rais, a harmless little bunny.

13. You can always find something to hold against somebody, and with good reason. Even so, a strong man is so unflappable that it's easy to hold several things against him at once: and thus all the more manifest. Refrain, however, from *offering* any objection.

14. Passing the age of sixty is no great joy and often a *fiasco*. Consider this when you're thirty, and don't be a tightwad with yourself. (What's more: a frugal man never wins.)

15. Whoever takes an interest in politics is not only someone who doesn't know how to enjoy life, but in some respect is also a cripple. Should you possess a sadistic inclination and dare not indulge it, then find another way to channel it. Doing so will allow you to satisfy this inclination completely, and safely.

16. The non-evident is the only thing that's really problematic. And whatever isn't evident is mostly not worth talking about.

17. A pathological burden is clearly no easy burden to bear, rather it's more a continual thorn in your side. Embrace it nonetheless and show the door to any doctor who tries to talk you into a cure.

18. The world is getting smaller and smaller. Don't ever forget this, otherwise you might think you're quite out of the gunsights when in fact you're standing right in front of the barrel.

19. Never dramatize. Always simplify.

20. When are you truly old? When having an audience is no longer much fun.

21. A competent person doesn't have run-ins with the law. More competent: someone who doesn't depend on it. Most competent: someone who never forgets that only government officials are able to skirt it.

22. A good listener is somebody who always and everywhere has an eye open for the horse's hoof.

23. When in public and blood suddenly rushes to your head, remain dead silent on every topic and smile at everything. Otherwise, you could stumble into committing a terrible stupidity that you'll discover you've committed only many years later, and by sheer coincidence.

24. There's a form of self-satisfaction that even the person standing by you finds off-putting.

25. No one can go full bore into life for very long. Just as many nasty coincidences as pleasant ones can happen to just about anybody. You have to know when to stop at just the right moment, if you don't want to go under. Obviously, this ends up throwing some folks from the get-go. Only a few, and rarely at that, manage to avoid pitfalls. Don't ever count on being one of these few, though.

26. No matter how strong you are, if you lack experience, you may perish faster and more horrifically than any ordinary fool.

27. Some pigheads can be unbearable, and you may end up noticing that even if you think you've left a fellow behind, he's still too close for comfort.

28. In order to show you're becoming ennobled, you need to be factual and independent in each and every respect. (Or, be *very* strong.)

29. If someone is speaking so slowly and thoughtfully you are amazed you're still standing there listening to him, then stay alert lest he say something meaningful (subterfuge!).

30. Over the course of centuries, intrigues have been spun into all manner of things they never truly were in actuality. This has

inevitably led to all manner of "wickedness." Turn everything into a banality and you will sow opportunity and reap success.

31. Not measuring time according to the calendar but to particular events throughout the year seems like a really bad joke. In reality, it is solely a question of willpower, the dimensions of which may be unexpectedly augmented by a great surge in one's zest for life. The inexhaustible reserves of strength found in those of a superior nature (rasta) often comprise such willfulness.

32. Whores frequently make movements when standing or turning around that at first glance give them away as a street denizen. Do you, too, have little quirks that reveal more about yourself than is advisable?

33. Being a coward is often the best way to save your life. Be brave only if something worthwhile hangs in the balance, and keep in mind that bravery is nothing more than the accursed wish to take up the fight in an inferior form, or to go against the majority.

34. If you've never heard the vitriolic confessions of an impotent man, his pathetic curses or mindless desires, then you really have no idea how good you've got it.

35. Should the absolute speculative nature of all ethics prove beyond retention, take a trip around the world. You will subsequently read Bergson and Spinoza as . . . as if you were visiting a home for halfwits.

36. Be very conscientious to speak of your private life in the same way you speak of others and everything else. Not least if you should be veiled in the mysterious, the uncommon, then in the long run all superiority (*on sait*) will not bring you that influence

you need for success (a sum). For all are driven by a clandestine aspiration for leveling. If you succumb to this, it will have succeeded, since everything and everyone has to be leveled. But if you deprive it from working on essential aspects of your being, everyone in turn will be plagued by doubts that they could have any success with you at all.

37. Don't allow your life to become too regular. You might end up liking it and in a year's time have a paunch and a kid to boot. Every decline happens quickly. And it's often the mighty who feel they're running headlong into it without being able to stop.

38. Don't shy away from occasionally being guarded and petty like any other citizen. Whoever conducts himself like rain does with soil will, without exception, suddenly find himself laid up in the hospital.

39. To be sure, your true nature is rooted in the soul of the desperado. But once you turn it loose, you'll have to forget all about it and become completely cold-blooded and focused.

40. Never meditate. Only devise schemes, prepare to dupe, and do not procrastinate.

41. In decisive undertakings, you may neither fully trust your experience, nor your reason, nor especially favorable circumstances. Rigorously test your plan, or at least parts of it, before executing it on the selected mark.

42. You will succeed over and over again if you never forget that it's not faith in and of itself that drives you, but a lack of respect for it.

43. Don't let success mislead you to setting aside the springboard of your inner tabula rasa. It is the secret of your strength and your victory. Should you come to rely heavily on yourself, and if you begin to have a positive belief in your superiority, when the time comes for the next vault, your approach will be skewed and you will come up short.

44. If overcome by rage, undertake some project immediately. If nothing comes to mind, then try explaining the power of moonlight to a six-year-old.

45. If you're still unable to humble yourself in the same way as you put on a hat, you continue to harbor a trace of false self-confidence.

46. Promise to fulfill every single thing asked of you. Indeed, promise it with such alacrity that any doubt the promise is sincere will simply melt away. Then, when you haven't kept the promise, people will have already so praised you that it's not even worth the trouble to assert the opposite about you.

47. The world is ruled by people playacting. *This alone is a sign that victory has been achieved.* Thus, never fight for anything. Perform for — *yourself.*

48. You can recognize your own boundless good fortune most clearly in the fact that there are millions of people in all civilized lands who actually believe one-fifth of what they read in newspapers.

49. Do not speak cynically too often. Whatever the case.

50. Never display even a hint of anger, not even once.

51. Speak ironically without smiling. Smile without speaking.

52. Display, as often as is necessary and without it being conspicuous, great amazement.

53. Praise others often. Be astonished seldom. Reproach, never.

54. Feel like a magician of the spirit, like a Fregoli of persona.

55. Your greatest advantage? Not being what you seem; indeed, not even seeming to want to be what you are not.

56. Trust, divulge to, no one.

II

KNOWLEDGE OF PEOPLE

57. Whoever praises life as beautiful and people as good is either a feebleminded fool or someone you're going to have to keep an eye on for a long time.

58. If someone tells you he's going to turn over a new leaf starting tomorrow, then you can be sure something very unpleasant has befallen him, perhaps even something tragic. Or, there's just a woman behind it all, jiggling her boobs.

59. As for any man who whets his knife only on reason, well, don't spend another second with him. Only someone who claims to be conversant with any topic could be of some use to you.

60. People who creep around like tigers incarnate are at the very least luxe.

61. No one is ever as inflexible as he makes himself out to be. Yet rarely is he as pliable as you'd like him to be.

62. Remember that anyone who has suffered at your side or spoken of their affection for you only gave you a vague feeling of impatience. You will then never make the clumsy mistake of letting others get involved in your affairs, that is, if you should actually wish them to get involved in your affairs.

63. People with thick-veined hands are not always old, but very often are even more mean-spirited and vain than cripples.

64. If somebody you are having a discussion with suddenly looks at the wall as if he were talking to someone else in the room, he is

without question under the influence of another strong personality (rasta). If you would like to break this hold, be aware that offering either money or other benefits will not untether him, rather, only the greater strength of your own personality (rasta) will achieve it. (More often than not, any incomprehensible behavior will also have the same cause.)

65. Whoever shows himself to be suspicious is almost always a patron who will prove too confiding and too gullible, and moreover a quick cash in.

66. If a loud argument is happening, perk up your ears. It is often just a quarrel (between the sexes) over hunger.

67. An easy way to get rid of obtrusive people is by telling them you're waiting for a bordello owner to whom you owe a chunk of money.

68. Anyone who harasses another is almost always ill.

69. The most dependable folks are those who ask a lot of questions and only answer you after two days. (No one is absolutely dependable. Anyone could commit murder in a heartbeat.)

70. If it seems like the voice of your interlocutor is cracking, either you have an opportunity or he will never have one again.

71. Whoever cannot bear the sight of blood having once bled profusely — is just weak.

72. The hatred of the weak is so variable that often you realize it only after having long since counted someone as an enemy.

73. Never seriously rely on someone who allows himself to become completely absorbed in a conversation.

74. If someone speaks about Buddha while lacing up his boots, you'll soon find you may have some luck in hitting him up for something.

75. People with narrow backs are clever, and those with broad ones are good-natured or blithely proud. Slumping shoulders indicate vindictiveness.

76. Whoever is really trusting is often a fearful coward — more often, though, simply curious.

77. Remain silent for a long time only if you want to poison the waters.

78. It is a mistake to compromise someone who wants to break free from his milieu. First compromise his milieu before turning to him.

79. Liars almost always become sincere when their imagination starts to fade. Don't let the passing of time vex you, and you will soon hear what you want to know.

80. Give no replies to someone who stumbles into a debate. Only the person who delivers a monologue will perhaps have something to tell you.

81. One whose mere look expresses a will to fetter and subjugate more often than not has already succeeded.

82. *Lacuna in the original.*

83. Should someone already be tapping your knee after the first few words, it will hardly be difficult to lie to him. But don't slap him casually on the hand in return: he may cease to believe you right then and there.

84. Domineering folks are not to be feared, only dominant ones.

85. If someone who's been silent for a while suddenly chuckles gently to himself, then the moment has come to ask him *the* question that's most important to you. For he will lie so imprudently that you'll actually have a palpable sense of what's true.

86. Whoever always knows the prices right away is a tightfisted scoundrel, albeit a very competent one.

87. Interesting people (so to speak) are always a little brutal.

88. Sometimes you really shouldn't listen too closely. You could lose the *other's* train of thought. And quite often, you might spare yourself the need to listen at all: just look him in the face, it will yield far more in the end.

89. If someone is already eating sausages and sauerkraut at ten in the morning, you can hardly hope to ever hear a single intelligent thing from him.

90. If someone's voice somehow throws you off balance, avoid him at all costs.

91. Whoever scolds at every opportunity, but doesn't look at all like the type who normally would do so, then he almost always truly means it.

92. Taciturn people are generally difficult to deal with. Don't deal with them at all: they'll regain their ability to speak at some point.

93. Irrespective of their pathetic little habits, many people are often quite sensitive. Don't try to explain away this contradiction — take solace and just shrug your shoulders. Above all, turn your back quickly on anything that at first glance appears to be

nonsense. By doing so, you'll have gained a great deal of time that otherwise would have been lost.

94. It's not an aversion to a world in which everyone betrays, sells, and swindles that turns someone into a recluse, but rather the fear of not having enough strength to relentlessly distrust everything, shadowbox with themselves, and plunder.

95. If you tend toward the eccentric, or the exuberant, then keep it private. The public would in no time find you puerile.

96. Anyone having just entered a room who wants to direct all eyes to him is either an actor by trade or a miserable bungler.

97. You can never, ever, put faith in boorish behavior.

98. If you can't seem to get a good read on someone, then try to imagine him naked. If this image shows him in a favorable light, then at least you've gotten a hint of what makes him tick.

99. If someone you've hardly noticed before suddenly does something that makes you want to meet him, then he already has, unbeknownst to you, taken myriad measures to achieve this end, and he's going to want something from you.

100. If somebody speaks to you as if he's gotten all his information directly from the mouths of the affluent, then ask him accordingly how much time he's spent in the clink.

101. Don't be too interpretive. Some people are much more thoughtless and confused than those we only suspect of having acted inappropriately to this or that poet.

102. Everything can be ridiculed. Only allow yourself this pleasure, however, with your lover, whose passion for you will only

grow stronger as a result. (Every woman harbors an anarchist within.) As for men, avoid doing this at all costs as it will impugn your character, and your friends will soon be ridiculing you.

103. Never underestimate the power of your surroundings. A conversation that gets away from you in the hall of a palace might have in fact ended with you ultimately prevailing if only it had occurred in a quaint café, and a woman who walks away from you might have been talked out of or into something in a bar. (This should make a greater impression than those details that have already made the rounds and are best ignored.)

104. Whoever appears especially pretentious is, in fact, sometimes just that.

105. Try to elevate the needs of those around you. The resulting satisfactions will in turn heighten your sense of life and — your chances.

106. You can't always completely avoid losing control of yourself (the foreground) for a few minutes, or sometimes even longer. Always make sure, however, to keep enough of your wits to prevent someone from getting the upper hand on you. (This is best done by quietly uttering a little cue to yourself when anyone starts to get the better of you. For example, "Luna Park.")

107. The fact that every man who laughs at you does so in the firm conviction that he's insulting you or trying to make you angry is a clear demonstration of how full of idiots the world truly is.

108. If the monster of indifference that you actually are could be visually perceived, you most assuredly would be dead after

walking only ten minutes. No man would be able to stand you for a second without assailing you with both fists flying. (If you get the urge to say more than you should when out in society, utter the cue "fool's death" instead.)

109. Prove something only when you're in the company of incredible idiots, professors, and newspaper subscribers.

110. Whoever speaks proper Volapük is never a respectable burgher — at best he's an artist.

111. Those who experience everything intensely are not suited for life and will bring you discord and losses at every turn.

112. Whoever would like to master men must never let himself be amazed by anything.

III

TRAVEL AND HOTELS

113. Whoever travels frequently encounters bad luck more often, but also far more opportunities than someone who doesn't.

114. Chance is no peddler, though it is always on the move.

115. Living is bearable anywhere. Yet definitely most bearable abroad.

116. The little mafias in every country are very powerful. This can be attributed to the fact that any native who would live as if he were an outsider would be totally ruined in a matter of a few months. People suffer the likes of you because you cannot be ruined.

117. When you're an outsider, every local can smile at you openly in the street. If you did the same, you would, in a matter of days — go missing.

118. The chauvinism and national pride of each country will show you how far each people are from being entitled to these two qualities. Only those who accept praise on the personal level and have no interest at all in either of these two qualities are entitled to them. (*"Oh!"* Right, but you can't say this.)

119. Always be aware that you can flatter almost anyone more quickly and easily by referring to their national pride rather than to them personally. Then you will travel comfortably and trouble-free.

120. It's often smarter to travel by slow train than to arrive three hours earlier. Or vice versa. To never err in this respect demonstrates mastery.

121. During a trip, remain particularly silent and unapproachable.

122. Large provincial towns are well suited to operate in, equally because there is little to do in them and because the distractions found in large cities are absent, and this enables your charm and ruses to work much more effectively.

123. Be well aware that after a certain period of time you will become conspicuous no matter where you are. In Genoa or Barcelona (for example) after four weeks at most, in Hamburg or Naples after eight, and in Marseilles, which is a particularly dangerous city, after only ten days. Only in Berlin, Paris, or London will it take about a year for others to become aware of your presence, should you frequent a particular part of the city or don't live somewhat as a recluse.

124. Paris and Berlin are your strongholds. Here you'll encounter a great deal of daring, intelligence, and intellect. You won't have it easy, but all avenues will be open to you.

125. Avoid taking a trip if a letter can accomplish the same goals. It's better to have a letter delivered by hand than to have too many individuals become aware of who you are.

126. Do not wear any jewelry in Germany, only very little in France, America, and England, and a lot in Italy. In Spain and South America, however, almost nothing can be accomplished if you're not sporting a diamond ring.

127. Always complement the dress customarily worn in a particular country with a small accessory that suits you.

128. Avoid hotels that charge by the hour. You will always be noticed in such places.

129. If you don't behave toward a hotel porter as if he has real power over your life, he will become your enemy. Big tips aren't always enough.

130. How you enter a hotel is unimportant. Hotel workers have certainly seen everything and even been fooled themselves about everything as well. Big tips will definitely generate more prestige than a coin hidden in a handkerchief. (Use several small suitcases, no large ones.)

131. If you are given a small room just past the courtyard in a hotel where no one knows you, then everything is in order. If, however, you are given a large, elegant room facing the street, then you are being mistaken for someone else, or they wish to keep an eye on you.

132. Don't fool yourself into thinking that the phone calls you place from your room or in the hall are not being listened in on.

133. Never sleep with a chambermaid. The next day the whole hotel will know about it and you'll be treated as if you licked the knife at dinner.

134. If you want to install a woman in your room, then avoid all the tricks of smuggling someone in and out, since it frequently brings unwelcome incidents whose consequences are far too unpleasant. Send your chosen lady to the hotel ahead of you and have her take a room on the same floor.

135. The chambermaid always knows everything you do in the hotel. Give her a good tip from time to time out of the blue, just to keep her in your confidence.

136. If you haven't succeeded in drumming up some respect for yourself at the hotel, immediately move to another and, if the city isn't too large, into another still.

137. If you are only grudgingly treated with politeness in the hotel, then others do not trust you. If you start to have a peculiar sensation, and it intensifies to the point that you feel the urge to turn around and look behind you, then you're being watched. If, however, one day it seems every third employee in the hotel greets you with a barely perceptible nod, then get the very next train out of there.

138. Eat in the hotel occasionally to demonstrate your sophistication. People might not think well of you, but they will respect you. Never eat everything on your plate, either, even if you're still quite hungry. Otherwise, the waiter will consider you practically his equal.

139. Keep calls to the hotel desk to a minimum. Otherwise, it won't be long before you'll be standing soaking wet in your room and needing to grab a towel. (This has caused many a man to miss the last train that ultimately would've saved his skin.)

140. If you've succeeded in garnering great respect in the hotel, you may then allow yourself, without worry, much more leeway than any established citizen would even dare dream of.

141. Never stay in a hotel longer than three weeks under any circumstances. You might be noticed. If you don't dare stay longer

than four days, make it generally known that you'll be staying for at least four weeks.

142. You can leave the hotel, too, if at six in the morning you hold under the nose of the porter, still half asleep, a telegram urgently calling you to London. By half past six you'll be sitting in the train and still only the porter will know, though not, luckily, that your telegram is weeks old and this is the third time you've used it for the same purpose.

143. Always leave a forwarding address when checking out of a hotel. (You might even end up using it later.) And also mention that a certain gentleman will be inquiring about you the following day and he should be told to wait another week, at which time you'll be back. Anyone who does inquire about you in the interim will thus be satisfied, or disarmed. And if he happens to be a detective, you'll even be bringing him a little mirth.

144. Decline hotel rooms with locked connecting doors, if possible. At best, you'll be kept from sleeping by noise from the next room. At worst, you're being observed or bugged.

145. Never enter any hotel room other than your own, unless you know where you're going. As to the fact that no one comes to see you, fabricate a story about a third party in a different hotel where you've booked another room by phone.

146. When staying in a second-class hotel, if the ownership changes hands, depart immediately.

147. Only discuss the most necessary things with hotel workers, but very politely. Smile at the chambermaid at least once a day.

148. When leaving your hotel room, immediately turn your back to the doorway and cast a scrutinizing eye around the room: you might not have closed your suitcase, left a letter out in the open, or forgotten to conceal a bottle of perfume. It's a simple fact, any hotel employee can open all doors and suitcases with the slightest effort by using their extensive collection of keys. Yet in this case it will be difficult to actually rob you. Even so: if you want to be entirely sure that something you wish not to conceal likewise doesn't get stolen, you must make sure to have it with you at all times.

149. If you are obliged to travel third class, pretend to be a traveling salesman. This is not only advantageous for the practice it affords, it will also enhance the élan with which you've imbued yourself when meeting the factory director shortly after arrival.

150. You will raise suspicion in Berlin if you assert that German men dress hideously and you much prefer cassis. In London, anger, if you do not eat impeccably and say you hate English cities. In Paris, disapproval, if you don't speak about yourself at all and get mad that everything everywhere smells like urine. In Rome, ironic cheerfulness, if you express an interest in the nonexistent nightlife and complain about the drafty bars. And in Madrid, contempt, if you don't love children and claim that, aside from the bullfights, there is really not much here of interest to you. Countries, too, cannot bear to face the truth and are more intolerant than some individual citizens.

151. If you are operating in a society where it is common for members of various nationalities to encounter one another, be mindful, if only out of sheer *courtoisie,* to say something complimentary

to each person about their nation. When in doubt, limit yourself to simply nodding or shaking your head. If the unfortunate circumstance should arise that, for example, an Austrian tells a Czech about all the praise you lavished on Vienna, whereupon the Czech mentions how much you gushed about Prague, you can be satisfied if, from that point forward, both simply consider you an absolute hypocrite.

152. As long as you are incapable of getting into a train car as you would step into a streetcar, you really shouldn't be surprised when the most important things fail to bring you any joy.

153. On trips, and in hotels, whenever diplomats, big industry types, and liftboys try to work their psychology on you, do nothing more than simply nod your head. If you are already at this level, the effect will be so overwhelming that you will have to be careful not to go stark raving mad.

154. In Switzerland, hate and envy are about half of what they are elsewhere. This is partially rooted in the psyche of the locals, yet to a greater extent in the bucolic nature of the towns and the absence of a true metropolis. Therefore, spend your vacations here, at least four weeks a year. (See also VI, 354.)

155. Always pay the first week's bill immediately, the second at the latest after three days. Otherwise, unpleasantries multiply, and often to an improbable degree. Also, never leave a hotel without having paid. The consequences are worse than if you had crassly defrauded a bank for a million bucks.

156. If you stay in the best hotel of a particular city and are still dissatisfied, then continue to stay there anyway, if necessary. Anywhere else, you would only find other things to complain about.

157. Linger in the vicinity of a hotel, no matter its location, only for a very short time.

158. Always use the elevator, even if you are leaving your room for good. If for some special reason you must use the stairs, still call for the liftboy as it will give the appearance you only used the stairs out of impatience.

159. In the Romance countries, never stay in boarding houses, always stay in a first-class hotel, never put your shoes outside the door, and have everything you buy delivered to you at the hotel.

160. Once a week, every week, castigate a gentleman in your room, behind closed doors, who in fact is not there, doing it so emphatically that no one in the hallways can help but hear you. And moreover, it will leave the impression that no one saw the unfortunate fellow leave.

161. Leave the hotel *once*, saying aloud to yourself, "*Jamais!*"

IV

WOMEN

162. Never get involved with the cast-off mistresses of other men.

163. Some women feel immediately bound to you. In some respects they want to give themselves the courage to say no, in other respects reveal they're not bound to anyone at all.

164. Many women who never have anything clever to say should in no way be considered stupid just because they don't have the patience to listen to stupidities.

165. Whoever cannot achieve mastery in matters of love by being an autodidact cannot be helped by any method whatsoever. Regardless, it's always important not to fall out of practice.

166. Don't presume to think that a man who takes a strong liking to the lady at your side has any respect for her because of you. If you want to be sure about her, you must be so lacking in respect that she in turn will respect you alone and disrespect anyone who has none for you, so that any other man will have no chance whatsoever.

167. If you're finding it difficult to convince a woman to give herself to you, then force her to spend three hours with you in a room without a mirror.

168. Only undress a woman when you have no other option. Complete lack of interest in doing so lets her know straightaway she's dealing with a pro.

169. If you wish to gauge a woman's attitude to her partner or husband, compel her to stand near him.

170. Is not a paid cocotte much more sincere than a wife who extorts you for a new dress in bed? (No matter how a sexual relationship begins, after a period of time money matters will always predominate.)

171. Women are always happy to be paid for ideas they consider their own; men, too, when they know full well the ideas are not their own. Therefore, only contradict women.

172. If your lover suddenly becomes very affectionate with you, then she's surely betrayed you just a few minutes earlier.

173. It's a mistake to believe that black-haired women are mostly just a little unclean, or blondes a little inhibited. Authors love to spout such aperçus since they seem so witty, and their prestige makes it hard for the reader to quickly notice that they've just read a load of garbage (a blague!).

174. The general idiocy of a woman can only be exposed by the person who discovers it. Some women are bright, some are stupid. Only the bright ones who lack any sort of imagination are useless in every respect.

175. A famous Frenchman once said that no woman would ever jump out of a car for the sake of a man unless she could hop into another. Never mind that no woman is ever so happy and content that she won't take a chance on a change of pace: allow yourself the triumph of refuting anyone prattling on to the contrary by the fact, and a triumph all the sweeter, that the woman, happy and content, has made you her change of pace.

176. A woman who doesn't wear makeup, although she could use it, is as stupid as one who struts around as if she were the most beautiful in all the land, and all because her abdominal condition can be seen from a distance. The only hope is that either might be worth the trouble.

177. Women who have an air of terrifying reticence are not difficult to approach; yet those who revel in the idea of themselves imparted by some smitten philosopher (ass!) are especially easy. In merely half an hour's time you can replace their delusions with a private performance corresponding to their true natures and your further intentions.

178. Only draw the attention of a woman if you plan to go on the offensive. Any gratuitous flirtation is forgivable, spurned advances, never.

179. If you want to remain a woman's lover as long as possible, make sure to be *this* too: her confidant.

180. Always arrange the room where you are to receive a woman so that it gives the impression of being somewhat risqué. Or, at a minimum, of being a monk's cell.

181. Only show yourself to the woman you desire on rare occasion and without approaching her. Even if she's fallen in love with you at first sight, she might not want to see you again after only one week has passed.

182. When dancing, avoid any conversation with your partner that requires her complete attention. Not only will your dancing suffer, but likewise her attentiveness to you.

183. You can gain the favor of a snobby woman by sending her a small Browning packed in a box of chocolates. Yet never forget to secretly take it away from her once you've achieved all you wanted.

184. If a woman asks you what's the safest way to prevent pregnancy, then don't waste another second on her. She's either homely or ill. (And rarely will your thinking be off about a situation in which much wouldn't have been accomplished anyway.)

185. If a woman kisses you without drawing a breath, or without a thought, then after three days you'll be able to have your way with her. Or, the next day she won't even acknowledge you.

186. Visit a woman you'd like to win to your side in a particular (non-sexual) matter during the day. A woman's influence grows in the evening.

187. Making a fool of yourself over a woman is only dangerous when desire overwhelms you to such an extent that it clouds your vision. In this case, do not hesitate to employ another woman as a palliative.

188. If not a single one of your methods has made any headway with a respectable woman, then spend a few hours in a barn before seeing her again. She will fall into your arms, stupefied.

189. Only a bungler or a skinflint would prattle on for hours with a girl on a park bench. He might have her in fifteen minutes if he would only take her to a reputable hotel, the elegance of which would simply be irresistible.

190. A woman who observes whores curiously and knowingly is worthy of your efforts. For the experience of the shabbiest and

most homely woman among them is so great that she may seem to possess real intellect even though none is apparent.

191. A woman of good society whom you see in the street daily in the company of a different young man has only one lover, with whom she will not be seen. If you want to have her, then you may neither speak of love nor try to get close to her via one of your methods. Eat and drink with her over the course of several nights, and tell a lot of jokes.

192. Do not think women who apply makeup to their nipples so that they shimmer through silk are easy catches. They may be very calculating, or very greedy.

193. If your lover is actually unaware of whom she has before her, then handle her as if walking on eggshells. Once she learns who you truly are, then she will treat you in much the same way. Yet if she suspects who you are, then you must absolutely make sure she knows the wrong version of everything. Then, if someone wants to learn everything she knows about you, they'll get it against her will, which in any case won't be hard to break, but it will be a false version.

194. Decide well between a lover who's loyal to you and one who will betray you. The former will only take revenge on you when she knows you've betrayed her, the latter only when she learns that you know she is betraying you. (This is being repeated because whatever one may *say* on the matter, this is just the way things are and always have been. Woe to you if you fall for gossip.)

195. Avoid having a single lover if it doesn't greatly interfere with your personal needs. Take one after another. Or better yet,

assemble a collection that can be fully replenished at any time, so that when you spend time with this or that one again, it will feel brand new.

196. A woman who loves black wool stockings and long skirts will never be worth the effort a sudden whim would have you expend on her. One who wears torn silk stockings again and again is either so desired that she has no time to put on new ones, or a complete slut. Either way, a capital opportunity may be developing before your very eyes.

197. Keep your hands off a hysterical woman, even if she seems to exert perfect self-control. She'll shatter that mask in a heartbeat, since you thought it impossible. Hysteria requires the greatest skill for disguise and is the most profound harbinger of meanness.

198. The most reliable way to recognize a hysterical woman is by how her facial expressions and tone of voice are effortlessly altered to correspond to the momentary situation, whereas a little effort is always required for others to accomplish this.

199. Only if it serves your purposes may you allow a woman whom you need to follow your changing instructions to focus on something other than her sexual relationship with you. Otherwise, one day she'll suddenly contradict you to such a degree that all your passion will have been in vain and you'll have to shift your focus elsewhere.

200. There can be no après for you. Your lover must be content that you've finally let her sleep, every woman on your list, that it's her turn again, and as far as the lady whose well-being depends solely on you, that sometimes you have no time for her at all. If it starts to go any other way, nip it in the bud, decisively.

201. If you repeatedly find yourself doubting whether a woman with whom you have important plans is fully devoted to you, then deeply wound her pride and take her hand. Should she offer only slight resistance when you take it, then she's really not yours after all.

202. If a woman seems completely unmotivated to talk to you, then you can be sure she wants something extraordinary from you. Go to her first to tell her you're having your stomach removed the next day.

203. If you're repeatedly convinced that a woman will never lie to you, then she'll want to marry you, or she wants to hear from you the truth about something important to her.

204. Do not dance cheek to cheek with a woman you've yet to bed. And if you have, still hold off at first, but only in the event she's become indifferent to you. (Very important!)

205. It often works well to dance with a woman you wish to conquer only after the fact.

206. You can have great success with lesbians if you remain quiet about their sexuality, as if it's a sacred mystery, and treat them with inscrutable discretion. (Same goes for homosexuals.)

207. Hook up often as long as it can be done surreptitiously. Yet never pay for it. After a while you'll have established such a far-flung network that your expenses will be cut in half.

208. Avoid compromising a woman even if your situation urgently calls for it. No doubt you'll have to put up with some suffering in these cases, but later (and it may be years) you will gain immense advantage from it.

209. If you're sure no one will learn of it, then sleep with whomever you want. Only let yourself be seen, however, with those women your most bitter enemies would gladly allow themselves to be seen with as well.

210. Make yourself the patron of all *bel amis* and *cicisbeos*. You will become so well and so quickly acquainted with those women whose affections would be of worth to you that you won't only get whatever you want everywhere with just a handshake, but quite soon, too, gain the reputation of a man of rare irresistibility and diabolical refinement.

211. Only bring women home by car at night. (Know your gemstones!)

212. If at some point it has to happen, only live with single women over forty. (Never with doctors, lawyers, professors, or pharmacists.) Don't sleep with their daughters, either.

213. Don't live with your lover. At most, live in the same building.

214. Never rip a woman's underclothes. The outcome is likely to be so negative that the next morning she'll be furious and by afternoon it will have impacted your designs.

215. Deprecate a woman's hat only if you know exactly who bought it for her.

216. Always criticize a woman's attire even if you're not interested in her. People will at least start to appreciate you. As it adds up, in a short time you will become a sought-after and delightful arbiter of taste.

217. Fashion may demand of you much of what its stupidity requires — always wear a good men's cologne when you visit a woman.

218. Absolutely *au fond:* only young fresh meat counts in love.

V

TRICKS

219. The impaired hearing of many people is merely a quarter due to physical causes. The rest is due in equal parts to a person's inability to understand what's being emphasized, annoyance at this fact, and the blithe thought that someone is speaking too softly. Do this, and his hearing will improve.

220. The good Lord is increasingly a poor remedy for the ailing. You won't get much further with theosophy. Tell someone sick dirty jokes, lewd anecdotes, and blame his past on nasty tricks. He'll love you after about a week, give you gifts after two, and write you into his will after three.

221. If you want friends to consider you spiritually deep without ever opening your mouth, then make a face whenever someone asks something sophisticated. People will believe you've had a particularly sublime thought, something exceedingly profound, and are too sensitive to say it. (If you have time to work it out, you might even create a literary reputation without much exertion.)

222. Some intelligent folks act stupidly, like an insect playing dead when a human approaches. The antidote? Act even more stupidly, and soon the other will triumph over you so brilliantly that you'll be able to recognize him for what he is and then have him in the palm of your hand.

223. Speak about what you'd like to achieve as often as possible in front of those who might be helpful to you. One way or another, their usefulness will become apparent.

224. A good way to get noticed by others is to act against them in some way.

225. If you wish to persuade a woman to jilt you, write a letter making fun of her and send it to her worst enemy.

226. If you are worried you might be suspected of something unsavory, stick your arm in a sling and say it got broken in a car accident. Everyone will feel sorry for you and drop all suspicion.

227. If a conversation takes a dangerous turn for you, then pretend to look for something you've lost under the table. When after a minute your head reappears over the tabletop, the danger will have passed.

228. If you've made no headway in becoming acquainted with a certain person you need to know, then let him see how you've fallen out with one of his enemies. That will win him over to you.

229. Everyone loves to judge. If you're afraid someone may judge one of your traits, then cleverly steer him into exposing this quality in another person. He'll forget yours, or think he made a mistake.

230. If you want to win someone over for a scheme that is altogether to your benefit but on shaky ground otherwise, bring it up while strolling through a bustling street. Your companion will only understand about a third of what you say and fail to catch the rest, even if he would like to understand more.

231. As for someone who lets you sit a long time in his waiting room, which features a yellowy mirror, do him the favor of making yourself appear unsure and sheepish. He will soon give his game away.

232. A fat boil is best lanced with a big kitchen knife. If anyone insults you in such a preposterous way, then give it right back.

233. If your hope was to frighten someone but have only managed to insult him, then act as if you were only joking. If this retreat fails, then go to ground, disappear, and never return.

234. If you suddenly find yourself short of something to talk about, then bring up — suburban pubs, factory environs, seedy boarding houses. Many things that are entirely banal and inherently ordinary become interesting when you talk about them (or write about them).

235. Should you need a scar, don't have one made on you. It could become unpleasant for you later. Point to the spot with your finger and say the wound was so expertly treated it's hardly visible anymore.

236. If you've made a new acquaintance, then after a week shout the cue "Venusgaze" and again mull over everything you've heard and seen up till then. You will undoubtedly discover improbabilities, contradictions, and lies. Its breadth will show you the right path to take, which otherwise would've escaped your notice.

237. If you perceive during a conversation that your interlocutor's only desire is to wrong you under any circumstance, then suddenly begin polishing your teeth with a handkerchief.

238. A good way to quickly get embedded in a woman's mind is to gratuitously give her a wide berth in the street so that she's left wondering if you were trying to avoid her.

239. Some people walk in such a way as to make it noticeable how long they've been sitting. Act as if you suffer the same problem, if

you would like them to agree to something anyone else would refuse.

240. In certain (mostly precarious) situations, the more advisable course of action is to forgo giving an apt answer; yet repeat the crucial words, the uttering of which now has a devastating effect. It's not easy to pull off, but can be mastered with practice.

241. If a discussion has reached a dead end without your seeing a clear way through, then execute a few maneuvers to create confusion. Your counterpart will turn and twist and reveal himself from unexpected angles. (The same holds true in relaxed situations.)

242. If you want to force someone to engage in conversation when he's trying to avoid it, then suggest a game of cards. Suddenly interrupt the second or third hand and ask a quick question. As he'll want to complete the hand already dealt, he'll give just a brief answer. Interrupt all the following hands in the same way, as needed.

243. Be frugal with paradoxes if you wish to cajole someone. But be extravagant when talking big.

244. Should an unfortunate turn of events force you to leave something to chance, then do not hesitate, when something even less favorable occurs, to turn and go in the opposite direction. A better opportunity can be found.

245. If you've given a false impression, then counter it with another false impression. People will begin to doubt, become confused, and stop concerning themselves with you.

246. If someone tells you that he saw you a few months back with brown hair, though in fact you definitely have black hair, then

ask him why he didn't come up to you then to convince himself.

247. If you no longer see any way out, then try whatever comes to mind. You might just come up with a fantastic ruse.

248. Whoever is being treated by a psychologist knows only one right way of doing things. And while you believe you're leading him down your path, he's taking you down his. When you've finally attained your objective, he still never really did what you actually wanted, but only, even in the best case, what was of no concern to him. If, however, you limit yourself at the outset to steering him so that he acts in accordance with his temperament and abilities, then as soon as everything lines up just the way you want it, you just need to give him a little push. And then, immediately, he'll do exactly what you wish.

249. If you are a sex maniac, and this forte is so overpowering that giving up too much lust for life would be required for you to modify your sexual proclivities, then ostentatiously *admit to it*, even brag about it. By doing so, no one will believe a word of it for years. If, contrary to expectations, it is brought up, then you have likely changed character, location, and maybe even your mania, at least a little.

250. If somebody says he met you two years ago in Rome, but under a different name, then reply that he's surely got a bad memory: you were using *his* name at the time. Decline to give further details while assuring him you would never do this again, if only he would try to forget your physiognomy.

251. Frequently ask anyone you deal with why they look so strange. You will hardly ever catch someone feeling caught out, but they will now refrain from doing you any harm.

252. Keep at least *one* apartment in a large European city, even if you don't use it for years, and a woman who, when you wire her, comes at once. Days later, you can sit concealed in your apartment and observe her by the side of a gentleman (in St. Moritz), whom she tells, acting on your instructions, that she has something to attend to.

253. If someone insults you publicly, then abruptly turn your upper torso and claim he's jabbed you with a needle. As soon as the fellow starts looking for it, call out very loudly, "Thief! Thief!" If several people rush to your aid, say you've made a mistake and leave the fellow standing there.

254. Should someone in your party suddenly appear intractable, then, if all else fails, the best remedy is to surreptitiously slip him a laxative.

255. Never carry a gun on you. You will be tempted to use it. One always gets the short end of the stick in such cases. And since the only situation where a gun might be needed is when your brain leaves you in the lurch, the best way to avoid getting into such a situation is not to carry a gun in the first place.

256. If someone asks you what's your line of work that allows you to live such a good life, then answer: "Yours."

257. Don't give your lady friends pet names, only seductive nicknames. While the drawback is that such names are a bit tawdry, they do have the huge advantage of easing tensions whenever employed in conversation. (Suggestive names!)

258. If someone has been trying ruthlessly to seduce your woman, then tell him loudly: "I'm aware you're no pimp, but if you travel

anywhere with this woman, sir, *you* will hardly be able to resist the numerous fantastic offers that will come your way."

259. A tried and true means of getting a snobby and overly cultivated woman into bed is to repeatedly give her the opportunity over the course of an evening to poke fun at your praise and admiration. Before everyone present. Afterward, remain alone with her and let her mock your praise and admiration, and allow her alone, among all who were present, to extend to you the hand of understanding. Very likely, she'll end up sleeping with you that very night.

260. As soon as you've gotten a woman into bed, wait at least five minutes before you begin. The longer, the better. This always works amazingly well.

261. If a woman is chomping at the bit to wipe the floor with you during a conversation, then give her ample opportunity to do so. Maybe she'll take notice and you can come to an understanding with her. Otherwise, let her keep believing you're an ass. This can be of use to you.

262. You can successfully ask a woman who thinks you're an ass to tell your girlfriend what an intelligent person you are. Cackling with laughter, she will tell her the opposite, and it will come across as so preposterous that she'll now become suspicious of you and will end up sleeping with you, even before revising her opinion of you.

263. If you want to keep a certain man away from a particular woman, neither sing her praises nor run her down in front of him. The best is to say in passing that you've heard the reason she has

such an odd walk is because she recently underwent a rather invasive operation.

264. If you crack a loud fart in company, turn to the person next to you and ask: "Say something?" (If choosing to remain silent is not imperative, there's no better option.)

265. In very doubtful cases, when it seems almost impossible to impose your will, the wisest thing is to let yourself go completely, to stutter, to complain. If you get a call the next morning, you have succeeded.

266. Never speak out in public, even in the unlikely event that you are forced to take a public position. Anyone who speaks out in public has immediately forfeited his superior position (rubber ball).

267. Always flatter prudently. *Semper aliquid haeret.*

268. If danger should unexpectedly rear its head in company, then, if other means prove unsuitable, start a conversation, launch into a vehement monologue that eventually erupts in feigned lunacy. As soon as the doctor arrives, calm yourself down, allow yourself to be led out to the street by him, and if he wants to commit you somewhere, give him a swift kick. Gone.

269. An invitation to dinner alone often gives the impression that you're interested in infiltrating. Some things are much more easily attained if they feel obliged to invite you.

270. To the extent your interests will allow, remain exclusive. Not only is this always shrewd, it has the advantage of giving rise to legends about you.

271. Should you begin to feel insecure in a city without being able to leave it, then go out for a walk while displaying a big belly. The authorities look favorably on a fat belly, and this is the best way to keep from being harassed. This will also affect you.

272. Go to the racetrack every so often and sit in an open seat and look at a wooden post in utter boredom. Folks will be talking about it in no time at all, and it will give you a great rep.

273. If someone urges you to tell your life story, always tell a different one each time. If anyone points this out to you later, act shocked that you're not being extended even the basic common courtesy anyone would have a right to expect. He will be amazed at your imagination and believe every word of your history from that point on.

274. If need be, make any claim you want. You can always disavow it later so that your prestige does not suffer. (Seam! Latheman!)

275. If you find that someone is telling you lies similar to those of another, you can be sure that both have received them from a third party. This will be proven by his telling you similar lies about the facts. (And if you're lucky, the truth.)

276. If you have no success in making someone believe something, then act as if you've forgotten to mention an important detail and then immediately remember it. Only now, talk about something completely different. After about half an hour, the other person will come back to the original topic, which you will then be able to make him believe. And from this point on he will surely have no further doubts about you.

277. Never try to cheer up a group of disgruntled people, but divert them instead with a discussion (about astronomy or airships). A boisterously cheerful group is not interested in anything serious, so instead smash a window, break a vase, simulate a fainting fit, etc. In either case, you will have attained the desired mood that will allow you to say whatever you want.

278. Always strive to get others to tell you as much as possible. Even when talking about matters the least interesting to them, they'll reveal more about themselves than if they were talking specifically about themselves. In the latter case, they'll always be on guard.

279. A highly introverted individual will reveal initial information about himself if you write him an anonymous letter. He'll either comment on it or modify his demeanor.

280. If you want to poach a dancer's lady, try to mystify him away from her side, without his being able to figure out later how it happened. Otherwise you'll have made an implacable enemy — *pour si peu.*

281. When you ring at an apartment, when your footsteps are heard, when you are seen from a distance, people must immediately recognize that it's you. In this way, you'll engender trust in others and can act any way you need to without anyone knowing who you really are.

282. If you need to refrain from involving the influence of a woman in a particular scheme you're pursuing, then this can best be achieved by completely ignoring the state of your hair and not shaving. If the *homme parfait* is also an *homme à femmes,* it will be rough going with men.

283. When in a group, run through your pockets frantically as if something were missing and state that you've lost a thousand mark note. Once everyone has helped you search for 15 minutes, pull the banknote from your vest. They will all breathe easier, talk with you for a long time about this event, and from then on it will be easy for you to be the center of attention.

284. Never repeat in the same city a con that's gone awry. And especially not one that you've pulled off successfully.

285. Give little gifts often. As a result, no one will be able to hate you very much, and those who cannot be bribed will still be somewhat influenced by it.

286. Only serious complications should cause you to light a cigar and sit down in a club chair. Everything else will then be revealed. Just relax!

287. If a melee breaks out, then only involve yourself if you're certain no one is watching. Otherwise, hold your belly with both hands and whimper and moan that you've been kicked.

288. Slander the man who slanders you, but ratchet it up a notch or two.

289. Never defend yourself. Be tired.

290. A conversation during which you were unable to introduce a ruse will not have told you much. Yet if several have hit the mark, count on the mistrust of your victim: immediately lament how impossible it is to really get to know others.

291. Be somewhat self-deprecating. If the person ignores it and talks about something else, you've failed. If, however, you're told

you are being unfair to yourself, then you know what that person thinks of you — or wants from you.

292. Praise yourself a little, but be prudent about it. If someone overhears you, then you've succeeded. If someone shares self-praise as prudently as you, then believe the opposite. If someone heaps praise on you, then perhaps he has actually fallen for your prudent self-praise.

293. Commiserate in some way with a woman. If she refuses it and speaks of something else, then it's succeeded. If she tells you that she is indeed someone to be pitied, then this is not the case. But if she wants to know what motivated you to do this, then it's failed.

294. Make a disparaging remark about an acquaintance's wife. If he ignores it, then he loves her. If he wants to know why you have made this remark, then he neither trusts his wife nor you. But if he says you're mistaken, then it's failed.

295. Make a disparaging remark about an acquaintance's husband. If she ignores it, you can have her. If she wants to know why you have made this remark, then she hopes to have ammunition against her husband. If she says you're mistaken, then she's neither interested in you nor her husband. But if she laughs coquettishly, then it's failed.

296. Prepare to leave at the moment you've managed to arouse interest. If you are detained with indignant words, then it's succeeded. If someone jovially pushes you into your chair, then he hopes to profit from a discussion with you. If someone lets you go without further ado, then he either envies you or is starting to hate you. Only if someone says indifferently, *"We'll see each other again soon,"* has it failed.

297. Remain sitting although all signs indicate your visit has concluded. If someone makes you feel that it's time to leave, or tries too hard not to make you feel this way, then it's failed. Only if someone is happy that you feel so comfortable there has it succeeded.

298. The last seven fragments should not only demonstrate to you the meaning of experience (in contrast to stupid psychology) but also persuade you to make a note of your own experiences. To each his own handbook.

299. To whomever you would like to give the impression that you have taken up his cause with all your energy, summon him to come see you at eight in the morning.

300. Should you want to compel someone to make a quick decision, and in your favor, summon him to your hotel room at eleven at night, receive him sitting on your suitcases, packed for travel, and make a blatant effort to conceal your impatience.

301. Don't consider someone who has said nasty things or spoken derisively about you an enemy right away. He may have had a thousand reasons for lying. Get to know your enemies personally and without delay. Often you'll find they make the best companions.

302. If all your tricks fail you in an extremely important situation, try, as the absolute last resort: crying! Men will be moved and women unspeakably flattered.

303. Tell yourself over and over not to use any subterfuges against yourself. Just endure, if you don't want to become weak. (Cue: "Bridge railing!")

304. Training is the only way you, too, will ever achieve greatness.

305. Practice physical exercise both in the morning and in the evening, the amount and type of which depend entirely on you. This is absolutely necessary for your body to retain its full range of motion and freshness. Do not participate in any sports whatsoever. It's too draining and softens the brain.

306. Don't regiment sleep to a specific time. Sleep as long as your body wants, be that fifteen hours or five.

307. Dreams enervate. They can be avoided by going to bed on an empty stomach and memorizing "The Loosening Song."

308. Keep to your little habits, even if they sometimes seem ridiculous to you. They will reveal a host of secret things you need.

309. Never get drunk, even if you aren't prone to run off at the mouth. The slightest high will damage your brain more than ten fine weeks of being in love. (*Never* be under the influence of any dope!)

310. Do not sing or whistle. Even if you're alone. It's like a damaging form of autosuggestion in the background.

311. Stand in front of a large mirror, often. Cast loving glances at yourself. Act up in front of yourself. Try to become more enthusiastic about yourself. Praise yourself. Be amazed at yourself. But scold yourself, too.

312. Know how to place value in the color of a tie, in the scent of a fragrance, and, above all, in the weather.

313. You can best free yourself from the adverse influence of foul weather by mindfully selecting your rooms and keeping your back to the windows; moreover, never go anywhere on foot and close the curtains in automobiles.

314. Many things can only be done successfully when the sun is shining. And some things should not be undertaken at a temperature of 5 degrees Réaumur.

315. Monitor the size and quality of your meals with the greatest precision. Should you eat soft-boiled winter potatoes and, even worse, too many of them, then you shouldn't be surprised when everything goes wrong for you on that particular day.

316. Avoid pasta completely, white bread, flour products, tea and beer, and all types of legumes. Eat only a *little meat* (never fatty), but plenty of *fruit, salads,* and *green vegetables*. Breathe deeply quite often, only bathe twice weekly (ten minutes, lukewarm) and every fourth day omit a main meal completely. Restrict yourself to *two cups of good coffee, four glasses of wine,* and *eight cigarettes,* or three cigars, per day.

317. Take walks often. (Everyone scurries around in their hundreds of thousands and you can see from a hundred meters they have no time.) Take your time with everything you do. Acting in haste serves no good purpose.

318. Live for yourself, insofar as possible, consistently.

319. Do, *in venere,* whatever you need to do. Fast once every six days throughout the month.

320. Excesses are necessary from time to time. After two months of unremitting consistency, your body will have had enough. Treat it to a brief but intense jolt.

321. However much you're able to boost your élan and bring about success through training, sometimes both are achieved only through excessive exertion. A gourmet feast or an unbridled love frenzy often might still galvanize you only if your training regimen has already been exhausted.

322. Practice persistence when dealing with people in the same way you would teach a dog a difficult trick. After about a week you'll soon notice that you can repeat the same question ten times in an hour without changing the intonation or sensing even the slightest impatience.

323. Practice your gaze daily while standing in front of a mirror. Your eyes must be trained to keep still and fixed on the other person, to quickly veil you, to sting, and to complain. Or, to exude so much experience and knowledge that your counterpart extends his hand to you in fear.

324. If your eye happens to wrongly stray on occasion without your having an opportunity to correct the mistake, then leave the scene immediately. There's no hope in salvaging this one.

325. The difference between virtuoso pretense and authenticity is immeasurably small. It can be achieved only through intensive practice, through which you likewise develop the ability to recognize authenticity. But if sometimes you're still unable to recognize it, then forgo any pretense (the major muddle!) and say what you are not at liberty to portray.

326. Though some ill-advised or faux mimicry will be less dangerous to you than an eye, it can compel you to sacrifice ten days where two would have sufficed. And this in itself might become quite dangerous for you.

327. Only when you have perfected everything that constitutes you will you have reduced all danger to a minimum. (Sure, sure. Just don't forget it.)

328. Always have a hand mirror on you. Once in a while you might have to rush off to the bathroom to try out a facial expression; or you may have to give your attention to a just discovered tooth cavity by scrutinizing it with a wall mirror.

329. Don't concern yourself with psychoanalysis, politics, literature, or science. They will rob you of time and energy while giving you no boost at all.

330. Read the politics section of the newspaper from time to time to spur you on from comedy to comedy to comedy — to comedy.

331. Keep away from magazines of any sort. They are more cleverly and intelligently put together than the newspapers and therefore capable of turning thousands of the young into idiots and making you — tired.

332. Never go to the theater. You'll ruin your act.

333. Spend time around married couples going through a divorce as often as possible. You will pick up a great deal for your act here.

334. Make sure that wit remains the most important rite in your circle, yet only when it's lively, spontaneously springing from the situation, the conversation, never preconceived. This type paralyzes, the other revitalizes.

335. Turn your wit on yourself as well. It functions as a spiritual purgative. Yet absolutely avoid this outside your circle. Your jokes would soon be at your expense — made about you.

336. Always prefer to go abroad since fewer obligations can be imposed on you. (Even clutter is debilitating.) And as far as your rights are concerned, they're lousily protected no matter where you go.

337. Never display hatred for anything. (Besides, concealed hatred is invigorating.) If the number of your enemies becomes too great, show contempt: it will make those whose hatred is constituted mostly of envy to assume it would be dangerous to awaken your hatred. In those cases, however, when you do have to let it show, let it coincide with action.

338. Speak more in a conventional rather than a principled manner if you want to gain time, and more chatty than informative if you want to gain the upper hand.

339. Never spend a second longer than necessary with genuine idiots. They tend to have a deleterious effect on the bowels. Doesn't every dolt look old no matter what his age?

340. Do not deal with utterly passive people. After a week, you'll feel like a scorched crater. If you're not able to quickly transform their lethargy into an easy mark, get the heck out of there.

341. *Lacuna in the original.*

342. Avoid people who live in such a hothouse atmosphere that you feel an overwhelming thirst for fresh water. And actually drink a glass as soon as you've gotten away from them. You'll never think of them again.

343. Only someone who's been shot at without result knows the exhilaration of pummeling a woman. Seeking danger betrays a weakened instinct: if avoided, your awareness of life, sexual powers, and sensory acuteness are intensified. (Danger as an opiate.)

344. If suddenly you no longer have the strength to lie, at least be cruel.

345. Never have a sidekick. Not only will he drain your wallet, but your strength along with it.

346. Wait as long as possible before employing a certain tactic that will attain your objective the most quickly. Any haste requires a great expenditure of energy.

347. If you're not attractive then it will be twice as hard for you no matter where you go. But more often than not you'll be able to conserve half your energy if you have a beautiful companion at your side, who, if necessary, could take your place.

348. When all the threads of the net you've woven start to come undone, grab them with your hands. And if this too should fail, know that you must be strong enough to abandon all of it with a light heart, to permit yourself anything.

349. No matter how definitively you feel immune to praise and reproach, there is always the danger of a relapse. Sensing that praise or reproach is having an effect, you can forestall it by shouting to yourself the cue: "Use the pasture!" This will immediately stiffen your resolve. (Grin, but don't anoint yourself. Napoleon lost the Battle of Leipzig and the Russian campaign the moment he had himself crowned in Notre-Dame.)

350. The danger of relapsing into self-assurance can be gauged by the degree to which your ability to disguise yourself is impaired. There's only one way to retain this ability undiminished: to exorcise your self-assurance again and again. ("Use the pasture!") Once it's been completely rooted out, it will reappear in a new, more positive form: The indivisible harmony of your pretense.

351. In everything you do, carefully gauge whether the inevitable downside for you outweighs the upside to such a degree that you will personally suffer as a result. Don't let your wishes or desires dupe you.

352. Don't dance too often. Dance only for your own amusement, or on special occasions.

353. Always have schemes in motion. One day you will suddenly bring one to fruition that has ripened within you almost without your being aware of it.

354. Your head works even without wanting to. You'll notice this most clearly once having spent four weeks in some small, boring spa town. Suddenly, you're a fount of plans and ideas.

355. If you speak with a hundred different people from morning to night, then after a few weeks you'll find that it takes a few seconds to remember what your name is. (This is by no means a joke.) If you've been using a fake name, this can be a real catastrophe. And it will always ruin your good form.

356. Avoid spending any time with the sick. Every sick person is the personification of misfortune. And every misfortune engenders vile ideas. (It is quite another thing if you just happen to *hear* about some misfortune.)

357. If you get sick, go into hiding. It will help you recuperate faster.

358. Shake hands with others so lightly that no pressure is felt. And do so as rarely as possible.

359. Greet others with your eyes or with a smile. Never with your mouth.

360. Never lean back in your chair while speaking. It impairs your thinking and your pronunciation.

361. Do not improvise when it comes to important matters. Do not undertake journeys on a whim. Never change hotels or cities without a compelling reason. You will be forced to make abrupt decisions so often anyway that anything more is a luxury you cannot afford. Moreover, it is often dangerous, and never free of stress.

362. Keep all stress to a minimum. It ages you.

363. If you're nearing forty, start to show exceptional generosity. It will prolong your freshness.

364. Having a family is out of the question for you. (Relations to parents and siblings are unimportant providing you are not too attached. Everybody is in South America, or dead.)

365. Do not live with anyone. It will unnerve you without your being aware of it.

366. If you've managed to alter your appearance and marital status so speedily and blithely that you have to remain quite vigilant not to be mistaken about any obstacles that might arise, then you are what you should be. But if you lie in bed at 4 a.m. pondering what

you imagine yourself to be, cheerfully answering: *"Haven't the foggiest idea!"* — then know that this is just one more obstacle in the way. You would need to turn your tired eyes, large and impenetrable, to this questioner and let four syllables slip through your lips, "Teremtete!" (L.T.).

VII

INSTRUCTIONS

367. What is *"animalistic grace"*? An idiotic pleonasm, since grace is a natural state and therefore can never be graceful. Every animal is natural (huck huck pree pree), thus never graceful, thus grace is never animalistic. On the other hand, it will hardly do to be well versed in the sort of affected language you might lavish on any valedictorian highschooler in the heat of a conversation; every noun not set in stone must be made ironic, with a nullifying sneer beforehand or afterward, or by an affected register. (Cue: "Panzerputz.")

368. Men who are easily moved or inclined to get misty-eyed are mostly bachelors, having this condition in common with pubescent youth, menstruating virgins, and women who live alone for long periods of time. After coitus, tears are a rarity, or just plain theater. So whenever someone is crying, quickly move closer — the melancholic are easier to manipulate.

369. The umbilical cord is a fabrication. And not solely because the mother is certain of its veracity. Everything is out when it is severed. Even hereditary traits make you independent. When troubled by a pessimistic mood or a setback, always be sure to look for a genetic cause. Look for them in your personal failings, in the misalignment of fates, or in the strength of an adversary. Otherwise, you will suffer the internal damage of bad luck as well.

370. Never offer forgiveness. It seems arrogant. Don't speak *it* either, for it has the same effect. Limit yourself to *visually* forgetting whatever has happened in the past.

371. It is painfully ridiculous to see someone in a situation whose causes you very well know are fake. Don't enjoy this pain for too long, and instead deftly offer the poor fellow a kind word. It will bear fruit later.

372. Some people when seen in public make a show of bustling activity. Don't be deceived. For the most part they are either clever Jews late on their rent or a miserable snitch.

373. Money or kind words will not make you any friends. If you want to bind someone to you, then make yourself indispensable to him. Everyone could use help with one thing or another. Whoever doesn't need you (now or then) cannot become your friend.

374. The agony of life is never far away. It often seems so weighty only because the sensation of pleasure it encompasses requires delicate nerves. The surest way to console someone in anguish is by exaggerating the agony you are supposedly suffering. After an hour, he'll accompany you to a bar and pay for your drinks.

375. Don't fall victim to the sensitivities of others, who are liable to be so offended by any word you flippantly utter that when you take umbrage at their behavior they will never get over it.

376. Don't let any plan, any idea, become such an albatross that you cannot let go of it when it becomes untenable. Otherwise, you will also become untenable yourself.

377. In some cases, it is important not to be present. Absence is not merely a half death (a quarter fame), it is also a good way to eliminate inordinate hatred or envy.

378. Children are very often wicked, and liars. Best to avoid them if you want to get somewhere with their parents.

379. People who often suffer from melancholy have it too easy. Cheer them up and things will improve for you.

380. It is often certainly advisable to act stupider than the police allow, but sometimes, too, to demonstrate (of course only for a few minutes) that you are as bright as you actually are.

381. Beware of people who lie incessantly and without reason. They end up in jail, innocent.

382. Hunters are seldom bloodthirsty, but quite often they're gourmands, sometimes henpecked husbands, and most frequently misers.

383. Music lovers are terrible sex partners, and musicians are very weak-willed. (If music doesn't make you nauseous, it's better to become an official.)

384. It is a widely held superstition that a man of spirit (scoundrel) must look like a jailbird or in his final month of suffering liver disease. As a rule, the sex or the will of these superstitious types, who of course now look that way themselves, albeit with prevailing intellectuality, is fairly screwed-up.

385. If you sense that another person is especially eager to hear what you're about to tell him, then cleverly begin by talking about something else. After a short time, you'll see that it would have done you harm.

386. Never turn up your nose. Instead, display a bit of humility every now and then. Although it usually won't be believed either, the impression it makes is rather *insidious*.

387. Never say jokingly, "And new life blooms in the urines." Everyone would be convinced that you've only recently recovered from some illness.

388. If you get the distinct impression that your counterpart does not know what he's talking about, then bring it to his attention. If he still cannot see it, then make sure you do not fail to recognize such mistakes so belatedly ever again.

389. Whoever lives chastely, and for whatever reason, will stand by you best. Anyone who has a mistress will not let you down as long as he isn't deprived of her. But you'll have no end of sweet trouble with a *coureur*. (Don't you already have enough trouble all on your own?)

390. Even sexuality can have a destiny that is often similar to a person's. Therefore, never fail to inform yourself about the sexuality of the person with whom you're dealing.

391. Don't ever converse with drivers or coachmen, even for your own amusement. They're all rogues and blowhards.

392. It almost defies belief what gestures, faces, even grimaces people make in the conviction that you haven't paid the slightest notice to any of them. But understand correctly: they *always* act this way.

393. If you suspect someone of something, then you must immediately listen to him attentively and take note of the direction your suspicions point you. Only in this way can you perhaps get a

leg up on him. *After* a conversation, almost everything is a kind of arbitrary interpretation.

394. Lie about everything to anyone who's a stranger to you. If proven to be a villain, it would have been too late otherwise. And if not, you can always undo your lies later.

395. It takes mind and memory to fool many people into believing in a personal relationship with you. If you are deficient in this area, then don't bother. (Very rarely will someone stand next to you like the fox next to the wolf.)

396. Never ride streetcars, only take taxis. But make sure never to take the same one twice. Many a banker would not have had to file for bankruptcy if everyone hadn't been able to recognize his car.

397. Only use the subway in urgent situations. It's too exhausting.

398. Always do background research on anyone you want to make your associate. In it you'll find the key to all the secret compartments of his being.

399. If you still feel occasionally sheepish after reading this Handbook, refrain from rereading it. It would be a waste of time.

400. If you have a handsome face, only one thing will prove difficult for you: the all too high expectations that it brings, so do make sure that you at least do not disappoint.

401. Always carry a few straight pins, safety pins, small nails, string, and a tube of all-purpose glue with you.

402. One of the greatest dangers you face is that a hundred inferior smart-asses (snitches) will create a composite picture of you

that matches you hand in glove. Though you can't prevent it, you can attenuate the consequences so that you don't fall prey to the law.

403. Always have a small Browning cap gun on hand that you can use to make a little noise if need be. In almost every instance, it should be enough just to show it. Should someone take a shot at you, however, jump to the left at just the right moment and knock over a small table or chair. You can often prevent the second shot by simply throwing the gun at your foe's feet.

404. If you've traveled around Europe a few times, take pains to avoid using the Volapük you might have a natural tendency to slip into when speaking. No matter where you go, it will be regarded as an affectation and you as unreliable.

405. If someone doesn't make much of an effort to conceal he's lying to you, then sometimes he is the best choice for carrying out some tasks to your satisfaction.

406. Allow someone to catch you in a lie. He will immediately try to rip the mask off your face, but this will allow you to easily make good use of him.

407. Never tell stories in any other way than by caricaturing. Only when you were part of them should you make it clear that you're not able to typify them. Then maybe you will be believed.

408. No one is so stupid that you can't convince him he's a genius within three days.

409. Don't speak softly for too long. It will be assumed that you've gotten into the habit for nefarious reasons. (Yet always talk softly on the phone.)

410. Respect the lifestyles of others who certainly will not respect yours in turn, but only so much that you'll be able to predict them and readily achieve what was uncertain.

411. The more extraordinary one of your deeds, the more you should take care to make it seem vulgar. If this should prove impossible, it is almost always more advisable to simply refrain from doing it.

412. Always manage your own finances. Whatever you lose through bad choices you would've been bilked out of anyway by a professional, who also doesn't always manage money judiciously.

413. If you're not yet over fifty, associate with men younger than twenty-five and older than fifty. Those in between despise you too much.

414. Distinguish yourself from others in everything you do. It arouses curiosity. But don't stand out too much or you'll just end up falling.

415. Be fifty percent quieter in an apartment other than your own where you have to be fifty percent quieter than your guests. Then everyone who is bored will just blame someone else.

416. It is popular to ridicule the unpopular. And it is unpopular not to find the popular peerless.

417. Be punctual. You'll always be early, but others will often show up too late: by then you will have already smuggled in directives.

418. If all sorts of rumors start swirling about you, deny all the damaging ones over and over, but halfheartedly. The flattering ones only occasionally, but emphatically.

419. One is never more thankful than for gratified pleasure, never more willing than for deft praise.

420. Give everyone the impression that you find women unbearable, have no children, and accept the prevailing political course.

421. Have a secret pocket. Learn hypnosis. Suddenly close your eyes every so often.

VIII

OF ESPECIAL IMPORTANCE

422. Wherever you may be, always tell yourself the following: *"Everything happening around me might also be an act."* By doing this, you'll retain good health and do rather well in this world.

423. Even a chimneysweep can be just a chimneysweep, or a charlatan. And anyone, anything at all.

424. The suspicion that he is confronted by a villain gives the upstanding citizen reason enough to start acting villainously toward him. If any such suspicion should fall on you, therefore, exercise twice the caution when confronted by those who administer law and order.

425. There is a kind of bird-like freedom that first has to be experienced before you understand what menace awaits if you take too long before you stop considering the State just.

426. If you continue to notice someone tailing you, check to see if his gait is a little inhibited, if he looks slightly pained when standing still in front of a shop window, if his hands are conspicuously still and yet take every opportunity to be moderately busy. If all this proves to be true, then you can be sure — he is no admirer.

427. A good rapier welcomes a worthy adversary. A specialist better makes for a dirty fight. Yet officials (of all stripes) to whom you don't blindly submit will bare their venomous fangs and bite you in the ass.

428. If the driver of the carriage you've just gotten into suddenly steps behind it, then he's either taking a piss or revealing your destination to someone.

429. If after leaving an apartment in front of which you've had a taxi waiting, and you notice the glass panel separating you from the driver has been lowered, take a different taxi at once. Do the same if you don't immediately recognize the same driver from before.

430. If the proprietor of a shop you frequent suddenly smirks when seeing you enter, then he's learned something about you or has been warned about you.

431. Always pay attention to the slightest changes in the behavior of those with whom you're in daily contact. The supersensitive barometer you've created for yourself can warn of danger in the nick of time.

432. If you let people know your intentions, they will betray you. Even if it's just by lifting a little finger.

433. Don't visit masseuses, unless you want a massage. Otherwise, you may be observed and photographed in the process. If it's just the common voyeur or private publisher, you can brush it off. (Avoid brothels for the same reasons.)

434. If you notice a conspicuous face in a restaurant observing everyone present, make very sure that those within earshot do not hear you speak. The sole purpose for that face being there is to mislead you.

435. If the customers at adjacent tables change at an unusually fast rate, remain silent or just leave the establishment.

436. If a gentleman with a puppy in his arms sits down next to you, watch your tongue and avoid becoming acquainted with the dog.

437. If a gentleman across from you in a pub is reading a newspaper with undivided attention, steal a glance at him when you pay the waiter. If at this very moment the newspaper reader happens to be looking at your fingers, you shouldn't be astonished at all.

438. If, in a buoyant mood, you once sung the praises of a certain type of sagacious, old black woman, and then someone like this shows up in your vicinity three days later, it's no coincidence.

439. If you've become a regular at an establishment and in short time two or three new waiters appear, then you've attracted attention.

440. If you suddenly start drinking tea mixed with red wine in the morning instead of coffee, and three days later a new acquaintance, who cannot possibly know this, suddenly recommends an especially fine wine and tea mix he himself has invented, get away from this fellow without delay.

441. If someone sitting opposite you in a café doesn't glance at you even once in the space of an hour, then he must arouse your suspicion just as much as someone who keeps smiling at you with unconcealed openness. A harmless fellow will calmly, briefly glance up at you six or so times during this interval. (This, too, could be a deception, yet it wouldn't be conspicuous.)

442. If you cannot avoid speaking to a woman on the street, take a moment to consider whether you're interacting with a lady or a whore. It is essential to ascertain if her questions are just as unsuspicious as her answers.

443. If you want to be absolutely sure that no one is listening to what you're saying, then avoid every pub and every street. Choose a freestanding bench outdoors.

444. Consider every ear within earshot as hostile. Woe to you if you should tell yourself, *"Oh, that's just an old man."*

445. If someone has eavesdropped on you while you were telling a lie, you can be sure that even if quite clever, he will think everything true just because he overheard it.

446. Always assume the walls have ears.

447. Never completely trust a lawyer. They're too involved with the authorities.

448. Never forget that even the most respected man gladly likes to please the powerful.

449. If someone who knows you're only available in the morning tries to find you twice in the afternoon (obviously without success), and only then comes in the morning, be on your guard.

450. If someone sends you a postcard that states he's going to visit you at three the following afternoon, and happens to run into you on the street that same afternoon, then quickly take your leave of him.

451. If someone is behaving toward you in such a way that it arouses your mistrust, tell him you're curious about him. If he replies that you're a mistrustful person, then you have a right to be.

452. Do important things in a hotel room only very quietly and with the curtains drawn.

453. There are people who pass you in order to capture snippets of what you're saying.

454. Women who peddle wooden beads in cardboard boxes never sell anything. Except maybe you.

455. It's better not to gripe about people shrouded in the depths of mourning seated next to you. Doing so might in turn have you in mourning one day.

456. Every tenth porter who graces a train station looks like a Nimrod in disguise. And that's what he is, too.

457. Anyone who presses up against you at a gaming table or in a crowd isn't necessarily a pickpocket. He might just be interested in finding out if you're carrying a gun.

458. If a gentleman picks up your cane, he's no gentleman.

459. If you keep noticing men with dark glasses, then you should not be too surprised if you're staying in Nice. In Vienna, it should make you suspicious.

460. If someone cannot read your legibly written name, then he can read much better than you might prefer.

461. You cannot deny that even eleven-year-old boys have the ability to mobilize their senses in opposition to your interests.

462. Only two out of a thousand registered letters get lost (per statistical evidence). If this mishap happens to you several times within a few months, don't chalk it up to bad luck.

463. Every city has hotels, mostly of second or third class, that are complete rattraps. It's difficult to recognize them. Take the trouble

to make a list of such addresses and verbally pass the information on to others.

464. Do not enter a building with no doorman on your own.

465. If an apartment is located on the third floor and you do not see a door on the first or second floor, do not enter this apartment.

466. Never visit anyone at twilight.

467. In all countries, the privacy of mail is a fundamental law of the land. Some scumbag's anonymous letter is enough, however, for an official to decide to open one's personal mail for months, and to have the recipients surveilled for months as well. Since neither correspondence nor even surveillance is ever completely discreet, everyone is at the mercy of scum such as these. (But not you any longer.)

468. If a woman is sitting across from you in a café and just like you is cleaning her nails, just like you scrunching up her lips, and just like you waving over the waiter, she's an officer. (Good, good.)

469. You can tell if a letter has been opened by slowly peeling off the adhesive surface. It's always clearly different from a letter that's being opened for the first time. (A matter of practice.)

470. It's easier to give the slip to a pursuer than to evade pursuit.

471. If you know you're being watched but are unable to evade it, then limit your dealings as much as possible, only making vague remarks and adopting some inane habit.

472. Even if you think you're completely in the clear, walk decisively as if you're being followed.

473. The classic means of *ditching* a tail: In the subway, jump out of the train right before it leaves the station and into another train going in the opposite direction; slip into a building's passageway and let the pursuer pass you by before continuing along the same route; hide for half an hour on the way and reemerge with different headwear and altered posture.

474. Your departure should always occur so that the first person you encounter only has about half an hour until your train leaves. If you can depart without being seen at all, even better.

475. If you want to make sure that . . . give one week's notice that you'll be vacating your room. If the great emptiness that suddenly surrounds you transforms into an amazing burst of energy two days before departure, then try to keep yourself *ditched* out of sight.

476. Don't loiter on street corners. It might seem you're looking for something there. Never tarry at house entryways. It might be assumed you have peculiar concerns or fatuous love affairs. But do go to the train station as often as possible. Others will think you have returned from a trip, or are about to take one.

477. Out of a thousand men, you'll only find three who are what they appear to be; out of a thousand women, about half.

478. Remain standing in front of shop mirrors often. In this way, you can comfortably observe what's going on behind you.

479. Never mingle with the crowd. Never, for any reason. Neither in the department store, nor on the street. Here, several dozens of eyes will always be observing you at the same time.

480. Where you do not want to be seen, rely only on your own eyes.

IX

MEN

481. To know men, it's enough to know yourself.

482. It is often impossible to gauge the caliber and scope of men who rise above the mediocre. Some personal information, however, is usually sufficient at least to keep from erring in what's most important.

483. Know-it-alls only occur around the ages of 20 and 60, the ages when one was once stupid and when one becomes so again.

484. Lechers are often delicate gentlemen and always amusing, but also real tightwads.

485. Some men are able to amuse themselves merely by looking at their wristwatch and then stop after five minutes so as not to harm themselves. For the most part very serviceable supernumeraries.

486. An utterly useless man can often be invaluable to you. You will have provided a service if you've managed to dissuade him from thinking he's a genius.

487. Whoever is at once both oil and water will always be, when it comes right down to it, half of one or the other.

488. Very quiet, monosyllabic men are most frequently brawlers, but they lack vigor.

489. Men of vigor smoke a lot and love whoring.

X

CLOTHES AND MANNERS

490. Clothes only reflect the wearer if it's too difficult to make any judgment otherwise. Even if you have reason to assume it's just some ordinary guy you have before you, in the interim closely examine his clothes. They might reveal something about him later.

491. Never say, even if true, that your tuxedo is from Piccadilly. No one would believe you anyhow, even if you produced the receipt.

492. If you're already wearing a topcoat, it should be at least slightly worn.

493. The rage for black horn-rimmed glasses, which are intended to bedazzle the mind, is certainly on a par with the full beards that turn thirty-year-old scoundrels into respectable fifty-year-olds. Renounce such childishness, which earns you less trust than a well-chosen and cleverly knotted necktie.

494. Only allow yourself to go out unwashed in very dangerous situations.

495. Be as flirtatious as required. Yet be careful that no one notices. (Exceptions: lingerie and a connoisseur of the absurdly grotesque.)

496. When selecting your clothes, be guided by your own personal taste. It will ensure that you have maximum effect so that not only do you feel excellent in your sheath, but also quite comfortable overall, because even what generally isn't agreeable is effective when worn well.

497. Seldom employ disguises. They always tend to rub off on you a little.

498. Never let nighttime be noticed in your voice; be unashamed of your complexion.

499. *Lacuna in the original.*

500. Only wear a flower in your buttonhole in the evening, carry gloves in your hand instead of a cane in the afternoon, and in the morning, try not to be seen at all.

501. Carrying a cane after eight in the evening is frowned upon.

502. Wear clothes that complement your basic body type, which you may vary with fashion articles that match your personality. Try to be somewhat out of fashion rather than minimalist.

503. Change collars and ties quite often, both in shape and color. (Repeat VI, 312.)

504. Prefer to stand in salons. It is more advantageous.

505. Make few gestures, but make them suggestive. Only refrain from those that are pleasing to the eye.

506. If your face has nothing else to convey, then always give it a faint gleam of pleasant discontent.

507. Be gallant to women, but only if someone else is nearby. It is more advisable not to be in private. Every woman rightly considers gallantry a little contemptible.

508. Be courteous to men, but do so slowly enough that they beat you to being courteous first.

509. Cough or clear your throat only if you really can't suppress it.

510. Never clap your hands.

511. Don't wiggle a crossed leg. It gives the impression that an entire school class has just triumphed.

512. Place great value on creases. But do everything you can to give the opposite impression.

513. Avoid smiling at women you have started to desire. Often place a hand on the forearm of men from whom you want something.

514. Everyone must get the impression that you don't realize you have a cigarette between your fingers.

515. Always keep your tongue in your mouth. This makes women curious and men well-disposed toward you.

516. Never play with your fingers for the sake of your lovely hand, never prolong a pose for the sake of your interesting profile, and above all, never gnaw on your thumb for the sake of your pearly white teeth. All of this is for a *vieux cabotin*.

517. Display an appetite when eating, yet eat neither with urgency nor with excessive slowness. The more routinely and gracefully you eat, the more often you shall be invited to dinner.

518. Always utilize a few small ploys at dinner that are new and can be performed to your benefit. This can make you popular more quickly than a two-hour conversation.

519. Under no circumstances should you give off the odor of laundry (chlorine) or soap.

520. Never wear silk shirts. Unless you hope to be a cattle trader or department head.

521. Always make the same motion with your hat when greeting. Only your face and eyes should deviate.

522. If you walk alone on the street, then your entire person (faint, yet distinct) should exude general well-being. If accompanied, remain completely neutral.

523. Only stop in front of shop windows that display women's or luxury items.

524. Never look at the sky or the ground.

525. Look everyone you speak with directly in the face. Yet only in the eye if you want to show benevolence, or — the teeth.

526. If you are assailed with a question, a remark, always act a little bemused — as if you'd just been wrenched from a deep thought.

XI

WARNINGS

527. If you want to change a woman's lifestyle or mentality, then look at her body when saying something crucial. But for heaven's sake, don't bore her with reasons.

528. If someone you're telling something banal to suddenly acts as if he's stifling laughter, then you don't have any ordinary flatterer in front of you, but a malicious hypocrite.

529. Always refrain from making negative assumptions about something with which you have little experience.

530. Proper gentlemen usually have several dozen coups arranged with their servants and chauffeurs. Once you have been fooled by one, you'll barely ever manage to gain their respect again.

531. Every city has hotels with staff who collude with professional criminals. (Before going to sleep, position a chair against the door with a carafe of water at its edge.)

532. A false name is more suggestive than an altered appearance which, upon closer inspection, is fairly obvious anyhow. In addition, the memory of faces is typically so bad that hardly anyone is ever recognized through a mask, only the mask, but then it's no longer difficult to identify someone.

533. Only wreck relationships between people if you need someone for your own interests. If you do it for someone else, things could get nasty for you.

534. Never act demonically. While you surely would be able to pull it off, it would be damaging later. The demonic has no real equivalent in life. So facts would inevitably leave you in the lurch. If you are who you are supposed to be, then you will acquire a demonic reputation anyway. This will be all the more useful to you when you have no control over it, but don't stop waiting for its emanation either.

535. Fear coincidence. It can be horrible. And it is more common than most realize. The best defense against it is to always be composed and in tip-top form.

536. Never let yourself be seen with a girl who looks like she could be twelve years old; but don't worry about being seen with an actual twelve-year-old who looks like a seventeen-year-old. Pretense is always everything.

537. To ignore pretense, you would have to be a millionaire, but don't expect to be one for long.

538. If you encounter someone who lives life completely indifferent to what his milieu might think about his words and actions, then you're either facing someone intending to commit suicide, or at the very least someone who's damaged goods. Avoid him like the plague if you don't want to go down, too.

539. Make fun of no one. On the most basic level, they wouldn't get the joke you're making about them anyhow.

540. Do not repeat yourself. If you've said something stupendously brilliant at three o'clock, yet repeated it twice over the next hour, everyone will be inclined to think you an idiot.

541. If dealing with a third party, you'll be able to foist the most unlikely things on just about anyone. But if the third party is an enemy, you could end up with a broken neck.

542. If you cannot develop the skills to respond quickly commensurate to any emerging situation, then forgo any kind of libertinism.

543. If you don't know to stop where bad taste and common avarice for lucre begin, then you'll soon rightly be sitting in jail.

544. Your ambition to accomplish the difficult, even the seemingly impossible, must have limits: namely, reasonable benefit and your health.

545. If your health is risked, the stakes are almost always too high.

546. Never act as if you are anything more than a big industrialist without an office. If you act like you're something more, you are basically committing blatant idiocy.

547. Do not undertake anything as long as music can be heard. It has a negative impact. Only venture out while jazz is playing. It loosens you up.

548. Men who have already gone bankrupt once tend to recoup losses with a single stroke. Get involved with such types only if you are able to restrain their recklessness.

549. Do not use a chess move that has already failed once. People won't hold it against you, but they will remember.

550. Don't throw any big parties. No matter how careful you might select the guests and make the arrangements, it will always

end in a brouhaha anyway. Be happy if nothing worse happens than someone emptying a glass of wine into the piano.

551. Only host dinners for four. Or two. Never three.

552. Always assume that whomever you are speaking with, as soon as you've left, will distort to others everything you've said.

553. Never litigate. This is not the way for someone who can appeal only to his own good sense of what's right.

554. If you're in the wrong, you still have a chance to win litigation. *Even the likes of you.*

555. If you happen to master several dialects, conceal this fact. The only way to acquire them is by spending time around common folk. It would seem improbable that you never associated with such types before. And it is, too.

556. Never let a sudden surge of joy catch you off guard.

XII

MONEY AND LETTERS

557. It is impractical not to write letters or to write only postcards. (In case of emergency, your handwriting can always be obtained.) For a letter is a more suggestive means than a telephone conversation, indeed, in certain cases even preferable to a face-to-face meeting.

558. Learn how to send a telegram so that it looks encrypted without actually being so. And vice versa.

559. It's not difficult to write down the actual contents often found in a letter so that it gives a skewed impression. (Repeat VIII, 467.)

560. A tried-and-tested method for achieving a goal is to fire off a dozen letters in quick succession.

561. It is more advisable by far not to clearly state in a letter what you actually want, but to limit yourself to creating an atmosphere that predisposes recipients to express what they want.

562. Work on the will of others by letter rather than by employing arguments to contradict them.

563. If you do not want to reply to an important yet very unpleasant letter, then let the sender know through a third party that you have suffered a hemorrhage and are in a sanitarium.

564. Spelling the first name of the addressee incorrectly and signing your name as if in a dream is not advisable if you want to give the impression that the letter is of no value to you. For this

purpose, compose it with the utmost meticulousness, yet undermine its content with some flagrant error.

565. Love letters are *the* epitome of stupidity.

566. Be neither generous nor frugal, and profligate only in very special cases.

567. Don't be too generous when tipping the waiter in a chic bar. Otherwise, he'll take you for what you are.

568. If you need money in your pocket to feel comfortable in the role you're playing, then force yourself to go out without a penny three times a week and overcome all difficulties you encounter. This will teach you to get used to it.

569. There are situations that go wrong if you pull money out of a vest pocket and go right if you use a wallet. (Therefore, always carry a billfold as well.)

570. Don't covet money so much that it becomes difficult for you, if the situation calls for it, to commit to doing nothing for many weeks. Many have come to untimely ruin simply because they could not quit the habit of dropping a few thousand each month.

571. Only take risks with money. Never your freedom. Choose to wash dishes if need be. It will do your élan less damage than four days in jail.

572. Don't hide the fact that you value money. If you do, others will only consider you petty or stingy.

573. If you meet a financier, immediately propose a business deal to him, no matter how fantastic. He will undoubtedly decline to

take you up on it, but will be sure to remember you nonetheless. And maybe one day he'll even suggest a deal to you.

574. More than just money-grubbing goes where money flows. Never underestimate the energy of someone chasing after money. Wherever this is going on three times in short order, you will often have trouble persuading a rich man to get off his ass.

575. When closing a business deal that thus far has gone smoothly, suddenly let your face display distrust. In all likelihood your opposite number will let something slip that would have made any hope of profits illusory if you hadn't made that face.

576. Refuse banknotes with private markings, or exchange them immediately.

577. Pay with gold pieces often. It will make you look wealthier.

578. Everything about you must always create the impression of affluence. Yet only rarely speak about money.

XIII

SUPERSTITION

579. If it so happens in the course of a long conversation that you and your interlocutor suddenly gaze madly into each other's eyes, there is absolutely no reason to consider it an ill omen. Rather, it is the moment you come together.

580. Displaying a weapon to a woman often has less effect than the knack for arousing her superstitions.

581. Superstition is the fear of one's own weakness and the hope of an external power.

582. Always precisely determine how every scheme is to begin and its final objective. As for everything in between, only stick to general guidance. Once in motion, the unexpected almost always happens. Yet whoever adheres to any superstition during this "in motion" phase will become his own saboteur.

583. Superstition is harmless, even fortifying, if it really does no harm.

584. Not using a calling card is a superstition as well, but first and foremost a very wise habit. Given that most people have better aural than visual memory, your name, if you have to repeat it over and over, will soon come to have a ring of familiarity.

585. Force yourself to regard the numbers 13 and 7 as no different from any others. Whoever falls under this aegis has succumbed to a childish phobia. (*La barbe!*)

586. Should you run into a former lover, don't get involved with her if she has since become superstitious. With women, this also indicates an altered mentality.

587. It is a widely held superstition that one should be a regular in a number of pubs. But, it's also just wise practice.

588. The superstition of not taking a trip on a Friday is responsible for the loss of more human life than a thousand other idiocies.

589. If superstition begins to paralyze your decisiveness, the effect is simply devastating.

590. Many a person has gone from superstition to experience. Many remain stuck in it. Firm resolve is the most important thing. (Only someone who has a *great* deal of experience will possess it.) L.L.

XIV

LAST NUMBER

591. To be sure, the world wants to be deceived. *And it becomes truly malevolent if you don't oblige.*

Geneva, August 1927

THE MASTER'S SONG

Constant is my inscrutable eye.
And my lips they are not idle.
And my firm hand does hourly
torment all too soon my desire.

Oh, how I love to lure the gold,
to wake the beast till it howls,
huddled in a bar alone and cold,
a joke for all eons to come.

Nowhere do I have a place.
Many a blank eye has me in sight.
Daily am I myself the stakes
and I win myself every night.

To empty the Cup of Fortune's wrath,
is my trade and my quest.
I will fend off any impending death,
disgust having risen in my breast.

Immediately after you have finished reading, you should order soup and eat it slowly. As soon as it is time for the champagne, have the waiter bring your selection to the table. Better to leave after the champagne and go by car to the one, who . . .

In any case, you should apply what you have just read with the utmost precision, insofar as it parallels current practice. Not only will you be amazed by the success, you will be . . . You will simply be! Teremtete!

And now:

Good night and *bonne chance!*

NB: After waking, you should memorize "The Loosening Song" and then "The Master's Song." The participation of a lady is left to discretion per the instructions elucidated in this Handbook.

In closing, it's particularly urgent that you don't hesitate in making these 672 fragments your own. Whoever hesitates has already lost. Only if you take up the gauntlet without delay will you be truly loosened up and become what you have always dreamed of: the fortune-seeker of your own body and life — Rasta.

THE MARCHING SONG

As a thousand audacious rastas
don't be too wild or too fierce.
For all it's sooner or later basta,
so please strive to be well versed.

Gentle question by the author to his newest proselytes the evening of this very night:

> "Will she greet you when you meet again?
> Or will she . . . ?"

Quick reply from the newest proselytes, right by the author's ear:

> "She won't greet you. But join me in silence."

Echo from far away:

"BRAVO!!!"

From very far away:

"COCK-A-DOODLE-DOO!!!"

Who was he, this man born Walter Eduard Seligmann in 1889 to an affluent Jewish family in the western Bohemian town of Karlsbad, Austria-Hungary, which was to become Karlovy Vary, Czechoslovakia, in 1918? The man Hans Richter called "Dada's greatest cynic, a pure anarchist," who in 1909 would go to Vienna to study law and change his name to Serner and his religion to Catholicism? Who was this man of mystery, whose life was spent donning masks, creating appearances, who adopted the ethos of the con man as his weapon of choice to wield against bourgeois pieties and was reputed to be an "international impostor and pimp"? We know that like so many young men from Central Europe he fled to Switzerland to escape conscription and the meat grinder of World War I. We know he was present at Dada's birth in Zurich and was considered by 1917 its most important theorist. We know by the mid-1920s he had published the "Dada Manifesto," a few volumes of crime fiction, and a novel, along with assorted poetry and other texts in avant-garde magazines. And then he stopped writing and disappeared, not a word more from or of him. Changed name, changed religion, changed city, changed country, even changed class. Who was he? The rumors were as rife as they were salacious, and then he was forgotten in the tumult of the 1930s and 40s. Over the ensuing decades, many wondered if he ever really existed.

Serner arrived in Zurich in 1915 and quickly immersed himself in the city's literary life, his writing soon appearing in the antiwar journal *Der Mistral*, which he co-published until it folded after three issues. He then started his own magazine for literature and art, *Sirius*, which he ran out his apartment at Stapfergasse 21. It lasted eight issues, from October 1915 to May 1916, and featured the work of such artists and writers as Else Lasker-Schüler, Ivan Goll, Hans Arp, Alfred Kubin, Pablo Picasso, and Christian Schad, who became one of Serner's close friends. Some passages that would ultimately become part of *Last Loosening: Dada Manifesto* first appeared in both of these publications. Suspected of being a fanatic Bolshevik provocateur and a dangerous anarchist, Serner was under constant surveillance by the police, who even took the rare step of assigning a specific informant to him. As a result, he was always changing address, more than twenty times, to elude them, so that not even his friends knew where he was living at any given moment. Yet he was also somewhat responsible for this predicament himself. One of his "blagues," or pranks, was to send a newspaper an anonymous tip (as Schukoff perhaps?) that Dr. Walter Serner was a Bolshevik agent and receiving "revolutionary pamphlets" from Germany. But the authorities, generally at a loss for how to deal with this gaggle of Dada madmen with an affinity for self-mystification and practical jokes, considered this information credible and promptly blocked his mail. A subsequent investigation turned up nothing incriminating. Many of Serner's recommendations in "The Handbook of Practices" draws on these firsthand experiences.

When Hugo Ball launched Cabaret Voltaire in 1916 as, essentially, Dada Central, Serner remained aloof, eschewing the stage and masked balls and baying at the ceiling. Yet over the course of 1917, he became more involved with the main figures of Dada and emerged as its most important theoretician, propagandist, and organizer alongside Tristan Tzara, with whom he devised a number of pranks as well as organized salons and other projects, such as collaborating on the first collective "automatic poems" with him, Arp, and occasionally Richard Huelsenbeck (a handful of which have survived), most often while sitting in Café Odeon in Zurich. It was during this period that Serner began to write crimes stories, employing a raunchy underworld argot as a stark contrast to what he saw as the hypocritical platitudes of bourgeois society being utilized to drive the youth to their death in the trenches. Zurich at that time was fertile ground for protesting the war and the phony values of the governments and industries participating in and profiting from it, ground fertile enough for Dada to take root, stomping and barking on stage as a natural response to the war's idiocy. Serner's "Dada Manifesto" was his personal response to the madness.

He went to stay in Lugano for a few weeks in March 1918 to put to paper the ideas he had already discussed, performed, or published over the previous years, what ultimately became *Last Loosening: Dada Manifesto*. In somewhat altered, augmented form, it constitutes Part I, "The Handbook of Principles," in the later edition. On April 19, 1919, Serner presented parts of the Manifesto on stage at the Dada soirée "Non plus ultra," and this sparked a legendary melee that culminated in his being chased from the stage and driven from the building (although this was relatively minor compared to the attacks he would have to endure in coming years).

The first twelve fragments of *Last Loosening: Dada Manifesto* appeared in *DADA 4/5*, the "Dada Anthology" (May 1919), the main organ of the Zurich Dadaists edited by Tzara. But it appeared only in the German edition. Tzara, who had been promoting himself in numerous letters to Parisian Dadaists as the "inventor" of Dada, had complete discretion over what appeared in French, and *DADA 3* in late 1918 included his French text "Manifeste Dada 1918," the gist of which seems largely to have been taken from Serner's ideas (then unknown in French), or as Germanist and Serner scholar Thomas Milch characterized it: "His [Tzara's] text appears as a short, stylish, linguistically and intellectually offbeat summary of Serner's thoughts." So by the time Tzara moved to Paris in late 1919, his self-aggrandizement had successfully seeded the ground with the notion that he was Dada's primary "founder" and theorist. Yet for the Zurich Dadaists, *Last Loosening* was considered the more important text. When Serner visited Paris in October 1920, he first went to see André Breton, who had published his manifesto "Le Corridor" in *Littérature* that spring. A week later he met with Tzara at Café de La Closerie des Lilas, which resulted in their falling out. Serner preferred to keep the matter to himself, and he soon left for Naples with Schad. And, too, the irony could not have been lost on him that he himself had plagiarized about 80% of his doctoral dissertation and in 1914 forged a medical exemption from military service for the Berlin Expressionist and anarchist Franz Jung.

In November 1920, Serner wrote a report for the *Berliner Börsen-Courier* on the fictional Second Dada World Congress in Paris, chaired by Dr. Serner. His connection to Dada, however, was becoming more tenuous, not least because of his disgust at Tzara's relentless self-promotion. Upon returning to Paris at the end of that November, he sent a letter to Francis Picabia in which he withdrew from participating in the planned anthology *Dadaglobe,* which was never published anyway. In December, he attended Picabia's vernissage at Galerie Povolovsky, and just a few days later Picabia, Georges Ribemont-Dessaignes, and Tzara jointly signed a letter to the *Berliner Börsen-Courier* that maligned Serner, calling him an "outsider afflicted by megalomania." Serner penned an ironic rejoinder and then left Paris, and presumably Dada, for good, joining Schad in Geneva. Eventually, Schad and others, such as Huelsenbeck, Arp, and Schwitters, would set the record straight that Dada had no single "creator" and it was Serner who had been the real intellectual engine behind its final year in Zurich. Breton later explicitly acknowledged Serner's contributions in his text "Après Dada" from March 1922, noting: "I have so far been reluctant to denounce Mr. Tzara's infidelity, and so I have allowed him to enrich himself with the talents of those who were absent and whom he plundered with impunity."

Serner was unable to find a publisher for his Manifesto until Paul Steegemann Verlag took it on as part of its "Die Silbergäule" editions, placing it alongside work by Arp, Huelsenbeck, Schwitters, and Melchior Vischer. Although written over those few weeks in March 1918, *Last Loosening: Dada Manifesto* would not finally appear until the summer of 1920, now accompanied with a band around the cover that proclaimed: "Herein is the only possible SOLUTION TO THE RIDDLE OF THE UNIVERSE," and further declared it to be a "Handbook for the con artist and those aspiring to become one . . ." Serner had indeed gained a reputation for being associated with underworld denizens — pimps, whores, petty criminals, scammers and grifters — but he was also known as a linguistic savant, raconteur, bon vivant, adventurer, and author of compact, nihilistic stories that explored the very limits of eros, solitude, and crime with characters who inhabit the inhospitable subculture of modernity while speaking a gibberish that mixed High German with a brash street patois in which language was reduced to a slogan, a watchword.

In addition to *Last Loosening*, Serner's entire literary output consists of four volumes of crime stories, one short novel, *The Tigress*, various essays and poetry in periodicals, and a play, *Posada oder der große Coup im Hotel Ritz*, which had a single performance in Berlin in 1925 and was so panned by critics it was not reprised.

By the time Steegemann issued a boxed set of his collected work in 1927, which included the now revised and expanded *Last Loosening*, Serner's writing career was in essence over. So in addition to being his most original work, *Last Loosening* is simultaneously his first and last book. He had reworked the original version, altering some of the text (perhaps the most significant was to replace "Dada" with "rasta," which carries the meaning of a "con") and adding "Preparation," "For Consideration," and the songs. Thus the original "Dada Manifesto" became "The Handbook of Principles," and a whole new section, "The Handbook of Practices," was tacked on. Contemporary critics, liberal and conservative alike, regarded this 1927 version as something of a testament to Serner's intellectual bellicosity as well as a genuine instruction manual on how to be a professional swindler.

Yet what exactly is meant by this "loosening"? The German *Lockerung* carries the meaning of "loosening up," a relaxing, of fetters, chains, even of discipline. So in this sense a "last loosening" signifies a liberation from the shackles of bourgeois morality to be replaced by a radical form of subjectivity, where the most important thing is not what you are but what you want, and if you cannot be honest about that, then you're an easy mark in the game of corruption and hypocrisy the world plays. To play with the world and not let the world play you requires that you stay in constant motion, keeping your identity fluid, always having in mind your objective, and if inertia does set in, then you need to disappear. So while the book's subtitle implies it is a guide on how to become a successful con artist, nowhere does the text explicitly encourage or condone criminal behavior. Deception and trickery are only a means to the end of *opting out*, not letting the world put one over on you. Serner's con man has no desire for riches, much less fame. He's someone who enjoys the amenities of the big city and the anonymity of the hotel, and he would be altogether harmless if it were not for his outright refusal to participate in the socioeconomic machinery of the bourgeois state. He is, in other words, a Villonesque wastrel, a nihilist, believing in and standing for nothing, since any such "beliefs" would be used to send him to the slaughterhouse of some war. Realizing that thinking yourself rid of illusion might be nothing more than another illusion, Serner's impostor is an amoral moralist, a radical loner, and *Last Loosening* outlines the tools required to maintain this modus vivendi. Yet more than that, it provides a whole anti-bourgeois ethos of life while acknowledging that something better is *not* on the horizon.

While Serner's crime fiction is written in a more standard narrative vein, even with all the idiom, *Last Loosening* is replete with idiosyncratic land mines that are particularly challenging to the translator. In his 1971 memoir, *Relative Realitäten: Erinnerungen an Walter Serner*, Christian Schad points out that Serner was intentional in his sharp divergence from standard prose conventions, so that even for native German speakers, the language of *Last Loosening* can range from perplexing to utterly incomprehensible, devolving (such as Part I, Frag. 79) into a litany of neologisms, puns, and obscure references to individuals, locations, or events the context of which not even his closest friends might have understood. For such lexical inventions as *"Schuffsteller"* ("swinescribbler"), or *"Lückenwut"* ("void-rage"), and many others coined by Serner to create a quirky and hilarious lingo peppered with dialectal oddities such as *"Wupptich"* ("verve"), a "translation" is offered, yet more often than not it's only a best approximation and is accompanied by a note to explain the wordplay in more detail, especially when an adequate rendering simply proved impossible. The objective was to approach the crux of Serner's meaning while trying to maintain the playfulness and even impenetrability of the original. And while much of Part I may seem like rollicking jibber-jabber unnecessarily extravagant for the simple objective of pointing out the war's absurdity, or even the inadequacy of language itself to express genuine fury at the war, in the context of the era, Serner's language is nothing short of spectacular.

Steegemann marketed *Last Loosening* as being written by a "notorious continental and international con man Dr. Walter Serner . . . whose address won't be found in literary almanacs but can certainly be found at the police station. He is an international impostor of grand style. He apprenticed in Paris as a pimp. There is nothing in his books he has not lived himself. Mr. Serner doesn't even mind one bit if you write this about him. He is the owner of large brothels in Argentina and is currently traveling the Orient." Such gratuitous sensationalism was not much help, though, and Serner was dogged throughout the 1920s by attempts to have his work banned for its sexually explicit content and its open mocking of social mores. By 1925, he had achieved such a reputation that he was constantly having to fend off attacks that went beyond just targeting his work on its own merits and veered into the ad hominem, often with anti-Semitic overtones. Another attempt to ban his novel *The Tigress* was made in 1931, which ultimately failed in no small part thanks to the efforts of such literary luminaries as Alfred Döblin and Ernst Rowohlt. Once the Nazis came to power in 1933, however, all of Serner's work was banned and the remaining copies of his books confiscated and burned.

After the boxed set of his collected work appeared in 1927, Serner no longer published and "went to ground," and not even his friends knew his whereabouts. All sorts of rumors swirled that he had completely immersed himself in the underworld and was now a criminal, an international charlatan and heroin trafficker, or that he'd split from the underworld and was now in hiding to save his own skin. None of it was true. He had just decided to become anonymous, true to his maxim: "The best book: the one never written." He married his longtime partner, Dorothea Herz, and they settled in Prague. When Nazi Germany occupied Bohemia and Moravia in March 1939, Serner and his wife repeatedly tried to leave for Shanghai, without any luck, and in August of 1942 they were deported to Terezín and a few weeks later "East," where they were both apparently murdered, along with the entire transport, in the Bikernieki Forest of Latvia and buried in a mass grave. Walter Serner was indeed forgotten. Schad's 1971 memoir helped to revive interest in him, and thanks to the research and editorial work undertaken by Thomas Milch in cooperation with the publisher Klaus G. Renner, a new set of his collected works was published between 1979 and 1983. If not for these efforts, Serner's masterpiece might have remained as obscure as his con men hiding in murky alleys, looking for an easy mark or an avenue of escape under the cover of darkness.

For their direct and even indirect assistance in preparing this translation and making its publication possible a debt of gratitude is owed to: Thomas Antonic, Radovan Charvát, Malcolm Green, Tanja Heydeck, Thomas Milch, Pavel Růt, Andreas Puff-Trojan, and Andreas Schmohl of the Goethe-Institut for generously extending the grant's publication deadline to allow more time for revising and editing.

Mark Kanak
Berlin, 2020

7   *Anton van Hoboken:* Affluent Dutchman, Anton (Anthony) van Hoboken (1887–1983) was a musicologist and creator of the *Hoboken Catalogue*, a comprehensive list of Joseph Haydn's complete works. He maintained close ties to the artists of the day, and Christian Schad (1894–1982) claimed he was Serner's "patron," though if true it would've been only prior to 1920. Having "arrived" in society and a habitué of bohemian subculture and art galleries, van Hoboken undoubtedly fit the bill of Serner's image of the ideal modern man who lived life to the full. He spent the years of WWI in Switzerland and while there also became acquainted with Serner's girlfriend, Marietta von Monaco, the two eventually becoming lovers.

9   *Part I:* "The Handbook of Principles" is a slightly revised and augmented version of Serner's original Dada Manifesto written in 1918 and published in 1920 by Paul Steegemann Verlag (referred to as the "Manifesto version" in the notes that follow where many of the alterations are explained). Serner called the numbered paragraphs "fragments," perhaps as a nod to early Romantics such as Friedrich Schlegel and Novalis, for whom the fragment was a literary form.

12   plafond: Fr., "ceiling."

12   *parents, primers, Bible:* Serner's wordplay here is on rhyming *Fibel* ("primer") with *Bibel* ("Bible").

13   Non, je ne marche pas . . . : Fr., "No, I will not march. / No, I'll march no more. / But I might just go to Canada. / Who knows?" (The last line is in Italian.) Here and below Serner shows his fondness for certain French ditties of the day.

13   Que les chiens sont heureux!: Fr., taken from the lewd erotic poem "Bonheur parfait" ("Perfect Happiness") by Théophile Gautier

(1811–72), here enthusiastically referred to as *"ami, ami!"* ("friend, friend"):

Que les chiens sont heureux!	Oh, the dogs are so happy!
Dans leur humeur badine	In such a playful mood
Ils se sucent la pine,	One sucking the other's wood
Ils s'enculent entr'eux;	While in mutual buggery;
Que les chiens sont heureux!	Oh, the dogs are so happy!

14   *Bernheim:* Likely a reference to the French neurologist Hippolyte Bernheim (1837–1919), one of the leading researchers of his day in hypnosis. Hypnotic abilities and the power of suggestion were important for con men of all stripes. The Manifesto version has "renowned biologist."

14   *rastas:* "Rasta" is derived from *rastaquouère* (see *rastaquouèresque* in Frag. 5), which came into Europe from the South American Spanish *rastracuero* for a parvenu or nouveau riche, while according to Webster's it refers to "a foreign parvenu," or a foreigner who makes dubious claims to rank or wealth. In common use in France in the latter half of the 19th century to denote an exotic con man or adventurer, it is one of the key concepts in *Last Loosening*, likewise found in Dadaist Francis Picabia's text *Jésus-Christ rastaquouère* (1920) as well as in the writings of Leon Bloy and Robert Desnos, among others of the period. Coming into German from French, it was particularly prevalent in the Berlin subculture of the day. Given its association with the con man, "rasta" for Dadaists and Surrealists became a symbol of official culture, which they continually ridiculed as merely a façade. Picabia became acquainted with Serner in Geneva in 1920 (when Serner was creating his own version of "Geneva Dada"), and this might have been an ancillary influence on Serner's decision (along with his break with Dada) to ultimately replace "dada" with "rasta."

14   *serve up aesthetics:* Replaces "columns of feuilletons" from the Manifesto version.

14   *to fix expressions:* Replaces "unleash cash flow" from the Manifesto version.

14   *peepshow proprietor:* Replaces "black Pole" from the Manifesto version.

15   *the Bois, La Villette, Theresienwiese:* The Bois is the large urban Parisian park Bois de Boulogne, well known as a den of depravity; Parc La Villette is in the 19th arrondissement; Theresienwiese, the official venue for Oktoberfest, is an open area in the Munich district of Ludwigsvorstadt-Isarvorstadt, near the train station.

15   *habilittantes:* A neologism following Serner's *"Habili-tanten,"* combining "habilitate" (as in European academia) and "dilettante," thus: "habilitating dilettantes."

15   *biogeneticists:* The term Serner uses in German, *"Biogeneten,"* is meant to be pejoratively sarcastic.

15   dieu merci: Fr., "thank God."

16   *interjections are the most apt:* Since interjections are immediate and do not rely on any constructed semantic system, for Serner they are not "disgraces," and because they are short and need no explication, they reduce the chasm between language and reality to a minimum. So Serner tosses them around in the text like the porcelain plates he mentions as a representation of the fragile, easily shattered bourgeois world.

16   *Sapristi:* French idiom akin to "good God."

16   *Paul Oskar Höcker, Dostoevsky, Waldemar Bonsels, and Wedekind:* Serner was influenced from an early age by the social critique and existentialist, anti-bourgeois perspectives in the works of Fyodor

Dostoevsky and Frank Wedekind; Paul Oskar Höcker (1865–1944) made a name for himself as the author of humorous stories and crime novels; Waldemar Bonsels (1880–1952) became world famous for the children's book *Die Biene Maja* [Maya the Bee] and is included here for his critique of society, less so for his anti-Semitism. Bonsels replaces the name of Fedor von Zobeltitz, a scion of a noble family from Saxony and the author of frivolous humor novels, from the Manifesto version.

16   *teremtete:* A Hungarian expletive from the Hussar tradition roughly meaning "to hell with it!" See "Swig Around the Axis" below.

17   *stylizing head:* For Serner, conceit (narcissism) and boredom are the driving forces behind all creations of the spirit, whether art or religion.

17   *prigheads:* Serner employs here the neologism *"Ethbolden"* for self-righteous, moralizing individuals. It is derived from *Ethiker* ("ethicist") plus the ending *bold,* as in *Raufbold* ("thug") or *Witzbold* ("joker"). Serner is perhaps referencing a lecture given by Kurt Hiller in Berlin on Dec. 9, 1910, on his idea that conceit is the intrinsic motivation for all ethics.

17   J'voudrais bien être bonne, si j'savais pourquoi: Fr., "I would gladly be good, if I only knew what for."

18   liberatio: Lat., "liberation," "loosening."

18   *arrivisted:* A play on "arriviste."

18   *Sagot:* Most likely a reference to Clovis Sagot, an art dealer whose portrait Picasso painted in 1909.

18   *superprimer:* Serner has *"fibelhaft"* for a school primer rather than the common word for it, *fibel* (as noted above), so it seems to be a mordant pun on *fabelhaft* ("marvelous," "fabulous," etc.).

18   *Pantopon:* An opiate preparation introduced as pain medication in 1909 by the Hoffmann-La Roche pharmaceutical company. William S. Burroughs wrote a poem about it titled "Pantopon Rose."

18   *C-clamp:* The German *C-Klemme* is a C-clamp, used here as a play on *Klemme*, which can mean a "clamp" or "jam," while seeming to metaphorically suggest the *constrictor cunni*, the vaginal muscles.

19   *Samuel Fischer:* (1859–1934) founded S. Fischer Verlag in Berlin in 1886 and in 1908 launched the highly successful series of contemporary fiction *Fischer's Library of Modern Novels*.

19   *absence of dalliances:* Serner has *"Poussagen"* (from the French *poussage*), a deprecating term for a casual (sexual) relationship that is also likely a pun on the German *Poussade* for "flirtation," "love affair," or "lover."

19   *Fragment 10:* Begins uncapitalized in the original, as do fragment nos. 25, 39, 42, and 56.

20   *L'art est mort. Vive le rasta!:* Fr., "Art is dead. Long live rasta!" "Vive le rasta" replaces "Vive Dada" from the Manifesto version.

21   *eromasoch:* With "erosade" below, neologisms formed by combing "eros" with "masochism" and "sadism."

21   *di-do-DTs:* The Manifesto version has *Dada-Datterich* ("the Dada shakes").

21   *express trains:* This was a favorite venue for Serner's erotic crime stories.

22   *bracket-twerps:* A Serner neologism combining *Klammer* ("bracket") and *Fatzke* ("fop" or "vain twit").

22   *swinescribbler:* Serner has *"Schüfftsteller,"* a neologistic rendering combining *Schüfft* ("swindler," "rogue") and the ending *steller* (from *Schriftsteller*, a "writer").

22   *airy:* Serner has *"luftici,"* tacking an Italianate ending onto the German *luft* ("air").

22   *Golgotha was child's play:* The Crucifixion pales in comparison to the carnage and destruction wrought by WWI.

22   *Gustl Pufke:* A fictional figure invented by Dadaist Raoul Hausmann (1886–1971) as the embodiment of the German bourgeois and petit-bourgeois who displayed an unconditional servility toward authority. Hausmann published his manifesto "Présentismus. Gegen den Puffkeismus der teutschen Seele" [Présentismus: Against the Puffkeism of the Teutonic Soul] in *De Stijl*, September 1921, having first presented it at a Dada matinee in late 1919. "Thomas Mann" replaces the name of Expressionist writer and pacifist Leonhard Frank from the Manifesto version.

23   *Ravachol:* François Claudius Koenigstein (1859–92), who adopted his mother's surname, Ravachol, was one of the most notorious and popular anarchists in France of the late 19th century. On being sentenced to death he is reputed to have shouted: *"Vive l'anarchie!"*

23   *sudation:* By referring here to sweating, or glandular secretion, i.e., transudation, Serner is implying a "spiritual oozing."

23   *Manolescu, Charles de Hoffmann:* A native of Romania, Georges Manolescu (1871–1911) was without question one of the most famous con men of all time. Posing as Prince Lahovary, with proof of pedigree in hand, and accompanied by underlings, a secretary, and even his own courier, he succeeded in pulling off a number of grand frauds. His memoirs brought him fame, and they greatly influenced Thomas Mann's *Felix Krull.* Manolescu outlined the principles and tricks of the successful charlatan: he knows his way around all metropolises; is expert in national mindsets; is a master of dialects, foreign languages, and social mores; is always vigilant; knows the limitations of his physical abilities; knows how to take good care of

himself and draw the opposite sex into his orbit. Though no historical figure by the name Charles de Hoffmann seems to have existed, Serner might be referring to Charles de Coster (1827–79), author of *The Legend of Thyl Ulenspiegel and Lamme Goedzak* (1867). Ulenspiegel is a trickster figure originating in medieval German folklore.

23 je vous salue!: Fr., "Greetings!" or, literally, "I salute you!"

24 *the Church:* "Chchchchurch" in the Manifesto version, which in general is peppered with stammered words throughout that were later emended for the Handbook version.

24 trucs!: Fr., a "trick," or "subterfuge." Serner frequently uses *truc* in the text for anything from a con or a scam to putting on an act or a practical joke. Hereafter it is rendered variously as "ruse," "trick," "con," "scam," etc., depending on context.

24 C'est la guerre!: Fr., "This is war!"

25 *yellow guard:* The name of the royal infantry regiment deployed by Gustav II Adolf, King of Sweden, in 1626.

25 on m'excuse: Fr., "Excuse me."

26 *masturbation of vanity:* That is, a manifestation of narcissism.

26 dolce f.n.: *Dolce far niente*, Ital., "sweet idleness."

26 *Tusculum:* City in antiquity southeast of Rome in the Alban Hills — a quiet, secluded spot, a pastoral paradise, like Arcadia.

26 *Cosmopolicretin! Culticretin!:* Serner has *"Globe-Trottel! Glaube-Trottel!"* as a pun on "globetrotter" by inserting *Trottel* ("imbecile") and creating an alliteration with *Glaube* ("faith," "belief").

28 sc.: Abbreviation for the Latin *scilicet* ("namely").

28   *sweet, sweet Mi!:* "Mar" in the Manifesto version, for Marietta di Monaco (1893–1981), a cabaret artist, poet, and dancer who participated from the outset in the Dada evenings at Cabaret Voltaire. She was, apparently, Serner's girlfriend for a time.

28   *feed vulturously with Geyers:* The phrase in German here is *"mit den Geyern aasen."* Geyer is a town in Saxony near the Czech border, and *Geier* is the word for "vulture." Likewise, the verb *aasen* implies profligacy and feeding on carrion (*Aas*). So Serner is clearly making a double entendre pun, which could have an alternative rendering of "feeding on carrion with vultures."

28   *the swig around the axis:* "Der Schluck um die Achse" was published by Serner in the November 1919 issue of the Dada magazine *Der Zeltweg*, edited by Serner, Tzara, and Otto Flake. This text would later be expanded into *Last Loosening: Dada Manifesto* (1920). An English translation by Caitríona Ní Dhubhgaill appears as "The Swig about the Axis," in *The Dada Reader: A Critical Anthology,* ed. Dawn Ades (Chicago: The University of Chicago Press, 2006), 58-61. The phrase also means "to hell with it" and thus is associated with *teremtete* elsewhere.

28   *Evening Glory Fizz:* A Morning Glory Fizz whose ingredients include both Scotch and absinthe.

29   Elle a un savon à la place du coeur: Fr., "She has a piece of soap in place of a heart."

29   je me tais: Fr., "I'm saying nothing."

29   *global man:* A person whose mindset is global, as opposed to the easily manipulated, non-subversive, non-global.

30   *the high idiom!:* As part and parcel of bourgeois etiquette, Serner is offering advice on how to survive among the bourgeoisie without becoming an object of ridicule.

31 *vitalust:* The neologism *"energeil"* in the original (*geil* is "lustful" or "horny").

32 *Gaia Afrania:* Generally, a persistent, argumentative woman; Gaia (also known as Caia) Afrania was the wife of the 1st century BC Roman senator Licinius Buccio. She was famous for always pleading her own cases before the praetor rather than relying on a male family member to defend her.

32 It's a Long Way to Tipperary: English in the original. Composed in 1912, the song was popular with British troops in WWI.

32 *An important rule!:* Cf. *The Philosophy of "As if"* (1911) by Neo-Kantian Hans Vaihinger (1852–1933), which asserts that human knowledge is based on "fictions," including the laws of logic, that can only be justified pragmatically. Later Austrian mathematician Kurt Gödel (1906–78) formulated a set of "incompleteness theorems," the first of which posited that no formal system can be both complete and consistent simultaneously, and the second of which maintained that the consistency of a formal system cannot be proven within the system. Gödel's insights called into question the strictly rationalist conviction that logical thinking reflects our reason, thus any notion that we might always rely purely on rationality in our lives should be considered specious. As such, human reason produces thoughts and sentences that are mutually contradictory and cannot be rationally proven, yet are still true within the bounds of reason, which is revealed in the light of paradoxes.

32 Tant de bruit pour une — occasion perdue?: Fr. "So much noise about a lost opportunity?"

33 *Sotades:* Greek poet of the 3rd century BC known for poetry that was distinguished both for its licentiousness and moral ideals.

34 *Narva:* A city and river in Estonia; Juan Suvarin is unknown.

35   *Cartesius:* Latinized form of René Descartes (1596–1650).

35   Chapeau bas!: Fr. interjection, "tip of the hat!"

35   *Patent Oil Urinoir:* Likely a response to Marcel Duchamp's (1887–1968) readymade object *Fountain,* a porcelain urinal signed "R. Mutt" and first exhibited in 1917. Patented by Wilhelm Beetz in the 1880s in Vienna, the oil urinal, or "Urinol," used oil instead of water for flushing, disinfecting, and mitigating unpleasant odors.

35   *verve:* The word *"Wupptich"* appears a few times in the text. Apparently it is Berlin dialect for "verve" or "élan"; Cologne dialect for "scatterbrain"; and a Prussian colloquial term for brandy.

35   shut up!: English in the original.

36   raté: Fr., "failure," as in a "loser."

36   *(Central 1098):* (Bryant 1098) in the Manifesto version.

36   Un oeil dit merde à l'autre: Fr., slang expression for cross-eyed, literally: "One eye says shit to the other."

37   *viennaworkshops:* The Wiener Werkstätte were established in 1903 as a production community of visual artists in Vienna that brought together architects, artists, and designers working in the applied and graphic arts.

37   *brokerquills:* Serner has the neologism *"Jobberkiele"* formed of *Jobber* (a stock market speculator or an unscrupulous businessman), and *kiel* (the shortened form of *Federkiel,* "quill"), in other words, a pen-pusher.

38   *puffball:* The original has *"Bowist,"* which seems to be a printing error for *Bovist,* "a puffball," but as Andreas Puff-Trojan points out in his notes to the German reedition (Manesse Verlag, Zurich, 2007), this could also be a misprint of *Bolschewist* ("Bolshevik"). Radovan Charvát's Czech translation (2013) has "puffball" as the more likely.

39 *mustashell:* Serner's neologism *"Mousta-Schale"* — *Schale* is a "bowl" or "shell."

39 *didnyaseeit:* Berlin dialect, *"hastenichjesehn"* in the original.

39 *Shpirit: Jeist* rather than *Geist* in the original, which is also Berlin dialect.

40 ma pauvre: Fr., "my poor dear," "my poor little one."

40 *drop of spirit:* Double meaning of *Geist,* the implication being that since these men are not having sex they might as well drink.

40 *Henri IV:* King Henry IV of France (1553–1610) is reputed to have had many mistresses during his first marriage to Margaret of Valois, and thus his placement alongside Giacomo Casanova (1725–98).

40 *no après:* Fr., no "after," here in this sense: The previous absence of any repercussions from sleeping with whomever one pleased.

40 *spirochaetan-virulent:* Serner's neologism derives from the Latin *spirochaeta pallida,* a species of flexible spiral microorganisms that cause syphilis.

41 *Jakob Böhme:* German mystic, theosophist, and Christian theologian, Böhme (1575-1624) was born in Alt Seidenberg (then part of the Kingdom of Bohemia). The quote comes from Böhme's meditation on the nature of angels in first book, *Aurora,* written in 1600.

41 béguin: Fr., a "crush," in the sense of a crush on someone.

41 *jettison the monocle:* Cast aside your present mindset.

41 bocher: A yeshiva student (lit. "young man"), but also a "bachelor."

42 *tabula rasta:* Clearly a pun on "tabula rasa," a clean slate. Cf. Part II, Frag. 43 below.

43 *syntactical steam:* Serner has the neologism *"Satzdampf"* a pun on *Sattdampf* (saturated steam).

43 *Perlimpimpim:* One of Serner's interjections; see Frag. nos. 6 and 11 and note above.

43 le comble du grand écart: Fr., "the perfect splits" (as in gymnastics).

43 Je m'en fous!: Fr., "I don't give a damn!"

44 déganter: Fr., "to take off gloves."

44 *Bayram:* Turkish for "festival" or "holiday." Little Bayram marks the end of Ramadan.

44 *talion:* Based on the Latin term *lex talionis,* the principle of retributive justice whereby punishment is inflicted in kind to the offense committed, as in the Biblical phrase "an eye for an eye."

44 *Passoskskaya:* meaning or person unknown.

44 papillotes: *Papillote* in German is a hair curler, but the more likely reference here is to the French candy wrapped in a colorful twist of paper that produces a bang when pulled apart — a Knallbonbon, or Christmas Cracker.

44 gasconnade: Fr., "fanfaronade," "swagger."

44 *Simeon Achselschweiss:* In other words, Simeon Armpit-sweat.

44 tripot: Fr., "gambling den," also generally a "dive."

44 *Phlogistic* crapule: "Phlogistic" refers to inflammation in pathology as well as inflammable, in the sense of the nonexistent combustible substance "phlogiston." *Crapule* is French for a "crook," or "villain." So the general sense here is that of a rather sketchy individual.

44 la blague: Fr., "joke," or "hoax," or a misleading assertion of the kind that was a popular type of Dada prank as practiced primarily by the "'société anonyme," comprising Hans Arp, Serner, and Tzara, with Richard Huelsenbeck occasionally joining in.

45   *A perfect contradiction:* Cf. the Löwenheim–Skolem Theorem as well as the Epimenides, or liar's, paradox.

45   *Semp:* Replaces the name "Fec" from the Manifesto version. Fec, the protagonist in Serner's novel *The Tigress* [1925; *Die Tigerin*] is a master con man and pseudo-dandy. As a symbol of apostolic morality, the index finger is to be supplanted by Semp (Fec).

45   Memento laeli: Lat., "Remember this, Laelius," an allusion to Cicero's treatise on friendship, *Laelius de Amicitia*.

46   Eureka: Published in New York in 1848 with the subtitle "A Prose Poem" on the title page and "An Essay on the Material and Spiritual Universe" within, it was adapted from a lecture Edgar Allan Poe gave on his intuitive conception of nature and the universe. It is dedicated to the German naturalist and explorer Alexander von Humboldt. The band put around the cover of *Last Loosening: Dada Manifesto* stating, "the only possible solution to the riddle of the universe," was most likely referring to Ernst Haeckel's popular *The Riddle of the Universe* (1899).

46   Sex and Charac.: Austrian philosopher Otto Weininger's (1880–1903) celebrated (and reviled for its misogyny) *Geschlecht und Charakter* [1903; *Sex and Character*].

46   *haoma:* a Persian narcotic elixir made from the Haoma plant sacred in Zoroastrianism.

46   *the passementerie trade:* Replaces "the photograph industry" in the Manifesto version.

47   *an assy Rhum . . . (an assignment, renown):* The worldplay here is: *"ein Poposten Rhum!"* followed by *"einen Posten, Ruhm."* *Popo* means "buttocks"; *Posten* is a "posting," or "job"; given the context, *Rhum* ("rum") is likely referring to the stage name of the legendary Auguste clown Enrico Sprocani (1904–53); *Ruhm* is "fame."

47   chignole: Fr., "hand drill," or "jalopy."

47   *galette:* A flat round cake but also a slang expression for money, akin to "dough."

47   *Charlot Chaplin:* Charlie Chaplin's famous Tramp character is called *Charlot* in many countries, and it is likewise a nickname for Chaplin himself.

47   *Gerhart Hauptmann:* (1862–1946), a German dramatist and novelist who brought Naturalism to German literature and was awarded the Nobel Prize in 1912.

47   *Kempinski:* Grand Hotel Adlon Kempinski in Berlin counts among its most famous guests C. Chaplin and G. Hauptmann.

48   *mascotte bar:* The French *mascotte* means "mascot," but is used here in the sense of the epitome, the very essence of a bar.

48   *Ch. Huysmans:* An ironic allusion to the rediscovered Catholicism of Decadent French novelist Joris-Karl Huysmans (1848–1907), author of *À rebours* and *Là-bas*. He became an oblate Catholic in his later years as described in his last novel, *L'Oblat* (1903).

48   Après moi, la blénnorragie!: Fr., "After me, the clap," an allusion to Louis XV's declaration "Après moi, le déluge" ("After me, the flood").

48   Sturm, Aktion, Fackel: Wordplay poking fun at the three most popular magazines of the day: *Der Sturm* [The Storm]; *Die Aktion* [The Action], to which Serner submitted work; and *Die Fackel* [The Torch], written and published by Karl Kraus (1874–1936), who was known for, among other things, his aphorisms, which influenced Serner's Dada Manifesto.

48   separate *supplements . . . (external feuilletons):* In the sense that all newspapers published the exact same thing, or even the blagues Serner and Tzara unleashed into the world via the foreign press;

"external feuilletons" is an allusion to Karl Kraus's refusal to publish feuilletons.

48 B.Z.: The newspaper *Berliner Zeitung*.

49 last *crap ever written*: Apparently Serner means to say that his book is "good" since it points out how "crappy" it really is.

49 *Fragment 59*: Does not appear in the Manifesto version and added later.

49 *blaguer*: From the French for a "joker" or "prankster." See note above for *la blague*.

49 *Lust*: A bastardization of lines from "The Drunken Song" in Nietzsche's *Thus Spoke Zarathustra*: *"Doch alle Lust will Ewigkeit –, / – will tiefe, tiefe Ewigkeit!"* ("But all joy wants eternity – / Wants deep, wants deep eternity." — trans. Walter Kaufmann) The German word *Lust* can mean "joy," "desire," or "lust."

49 *clausal leaps with your legs*: This is a virtually untranslatable pun on the German word *Sätze*, which can mean either "sentences" or "leaps." The implication is that one should stop playing around with language (speaking, writing) and go out and experience the world.

49 *müllering*: Georg Müller (1877–1917) founded a publishing house bearing his name in 1903 in Munich, and it became known for making high literature available to a mass market and cranking out around 1,900 books in fifteen years, reaching a total circulation of several million copies. Having published such authors as Franz Blei, Hanns Heinz Ewers, Alfred Karl Mayer, August Strindberg, and Frank Wedekind, as well as bibliophile classic editions, fairy-tale collections, and adventure novels, it merged with Albert Langen's publishing house in 1931 to form Langen Müller Verlag. Apparently "müllering" is a sardonic reference to writing an excessive quantity of words for commercial purposes to satisfy mass-market demand,

and could be figuratively rendered as "word-milling." Serner employs this verbal construct a few times below.

50 *Fixatoir:* Presumably an allusion to "fixation."

50 la barbe!: Fr., literally "the beard," a common colloquial term for "deathly boring."

50 *Excessements:* A combination of "excesses" and "excrement," thus something to be discharged, like phlegm, or bile.

51 *fiend:* Serner has *"Scheuel,"* an outmoded form of *Scheusal,* meaning "monster," or "abomination."

51 *runs riot:* The verb here is *exzedieren,* apparently more common as an Austrian usage and derived from the French *excéder,* implying "excess," or transgressing what is generally considered permissible.

51 *Joachim Friedenthal:* Berlin journalist and publisher of *Das Wedekindbuch* in 1914.

52 *Monte Salvatore:* Properly Monte San Salvatore, located in the Lepontine Alps above Lake Lugano in Switzerland.

52 *"Laissons la salade. Faisons un grand arrangement.":* Fr., "Forget the chaos and let's come to an agreement."

52 *ipsius generis:* Lat., "of its own kind."

52 *m.p.:* Abbreviation for *manu propria,* "with one's own hand"; the quote is from Hamlet, Act v, Scene 2.

53 *la purée:* Fr., slang for "misery" or "sorrow" (lit. "puree").

53 *pépère:* Fr., "cushy," "cosy," or "tranquil."

53 *Pas la peine!:* Fr., "not worth it," "don't bother." (See pun below.)

53 *a short — pas (la peine)?:* A pun on the French *pas,* which as a noun means "step" (i.e., "just a short step") and as an adverb means "not," thus *pas la piene.*

54   *Qui est là?:* Fr., "Who's there?"

55   *You are there!!!:* Here the German reads *"Man sei da,"* with *da* rendered as "there" in this context. In the Manifesto version it reads *"Man sei da da,"* which could be rendered as "You are da da."

55   *the most* glaring *lunacy:* "Glaring" here in the sense of "pure" or "lucid," which refers back to the "blinding truth" mentioned by Serner in a 1911 essay on Karl Kraus. Here "truth" is replaced by "lunacy," which is so glaring you have to cover your eyes, implying, per Radovan Charvát, that lunacy (an absolute anarchy of expression) is truth.

56   *Jacques Lebaudy:* The scion of a French sugar baron, Lebaudy (1868–1919) sailed in 1903 with two other ships to a strip of land near Cape Juby on the Moroccan coast that was still unclaimed by any colonial power, whereupon he proclaimed the "Empire of the Sahara." Supported by a few hundred mercenaries and artillery, he anointed himself Jacques I, Emperor of the Sahara, and appointed ministers. The French government issued a warrant for his arrest after a few years of this nonsense, and Lebaudy left North Africa for good headed to New York, where he landed in an insane asylum in 1915. He was ultimately killed by his wife in 1919 on Long Island, for which she was not charged, having alleged that he had wanted to marry their daughter to pass on his royal line.

56   *Footit the Clown:* George Footit (1864–1921), real name thought to be Tudor Hall, an Englishman who was a famous clown in France and a fixture on the Parisian circus scene.

56   *Pankhurst:* Emmeline Pankhurst (1858–1928), British feminist author, political activist, and leading suffragette who founded the Women's Social and Political Union in 1903.

56   *Sirius:* The Dog Star, the brightest star in Canis Major, and also the title of Serner's monthly journal for literature and art that he

published in Zurich from October 1915 to May 1916; the eight issues of *Sirius* showed a distinct preference for Expressionist texts.

56   *L.T. ... (Last things):* An allusion to Otto Weininger's *Über die Letzten Dinge* [On Last Things], a follow-up to *Sex and Character* that was published posthumously in 1904.

56   *Fragment 78:* Added later and not part of the Manifesto version.

56   *Fragment 79:* With its stream-of-consciousness and free associations this fragment is very similar to the "Gemeinschaftsgedichte" (Group Poems) written collectively by Serner, Arp, and Tzara in 1916–17. This type of composition was later adopted as "automatic writing" by the Surrealists and became a cornerstone of their work. The fragment is a significant expansion on what appears in the Manifesto version.

56   de mortuis nil nisi bene: Lat., "One should only speak well of the dead."

56   nemo potest peccare ab umbilico et inferius: Lat., "No one can sin from the navel down." Cf. Stanisław Przybyszewski's *The Synagogue of Satan* (1897).

56   *Hecuba:* Wife of King Priam of Troy, whom she bore 19 children, most famously Paris, Hector, Hellenos, and Cassandra. Because she lost her children in war and then became the slave of Odysseus after the sack of Troy (per Euripides), Hecuba is the personification of the most dire misfortune that can befall a woman. Cf. *Hamlet,* Act II, Scene 2.

56   *lace-curtain-layabout:* Serner has *"Storelüdrian,"* a neologism combining *Store* (in German meaning "net curtain" and in French "blinds" or "awning") and *lüdrian,* a phoneticization of *Liederjan* ("ne'er-do-well"). The French poet Francois Villon (1431–63) was

known for his peripatetic bohemian lifestyle and for associating with the criminals and prostitutes of the demimonde even though he received two degrees from the University of Paris and his adoptive father was well-off. "Lace curtain" was a slang term originating in the 19th century for the affluent Irish. Just as Villon's ballads are full of underworld slang and inside jokes, so too Serner's texts, and sometimes the meaning is just a guess.

57   *Porkopolis:* An early 19th-century nickname for Cincinnati, Ohio, as the city was a center for the meat packing industry.

57   *Mörike:* Eduard Friedrich Mörike (1804–75), German Romantic poet and novelist.

57   *deux yeux disent merde à moi je me couche de bonne heure:* Fr., literally, "two eyes saying shit to me I go to bed early."

58   *flaoutter:* Presumably a Serner neologism formed from the French *flatter* ("to flatter") and *flou* ("vague").

58   *Pilatus:* An allusion both to Pontius Pilate and a mountain in the Swiss Alps.

58   *la ritirata manquée: La ritirata* is Italian for "retreat" and *manquée* is French for "failed."

58   go on and . . . : English in the original.

58   *paprikacothurn:* A "cothurn" was a buskin worn by actors in ancient Athenian tragedies in order to look taller as well as a stilted form of tragedy.

58   *dimwits:* Serner has *funzen,* which is Austrian dialect.

58   *esquadrilles:* A neologism punning on the French *escadrille* ("air squadron") combined with the quadrille.

58   *beaucoup de beurre:* Fr., "lots of butter."

59 *Coupe Jacques Plombières:* A sundae made with Plombières ice cream and candied fruits soaked in kirsch.

59 *Fragment 80:* This was not a separate fragment in the Manifesto version. The preceding fragment ended with "astral valor like only Cherries Jubilee."

59 Vive le rasta!!!: Replaces "Vive Dada!!!" in the Manifesto version.

61 *"Du kleine Klingelfee":* Apparently an allusion to "Hallo, du süße Klingelfee," a popular hit from Robert Stolz's score for the 1920 operetta *Der Tanz ins Glück.*

61 *"Emma, j'tai connue au cinéma":* Fr., "Emma, I met you in the cinema."

66 *2nd Motto:* "Don't let yourself be told anything!"

66 *4th Motto:* "Love only me. / I really don't care, / main thing is, I'm alive."

66 *5th Motto:* The entire stanza is in Berlin argot.

66 *7th Motto:* "Impudence is lovely. But / Serner is — more! / (The Redhead)"

68 *Gilles de Rais:* (1404–40), one of the wealthiest and most powerful French nobles of his age, who as a commander in the French Army fought alongside Joan of Arc. Yet he is more infamous as a serial child abuser and killer, for which he was arrested, convicted, and executed in 1440. Cf. *The Trial of Gilles de Rais* by Georges Bataille.

71 on sait: Fr., "one knows."

74 *like a Fregoli:* Leopoldo Fregoli (1867–1936) was a famous Italian master of transformation who could rapidly change his clothes, voice, facial expressions, and gestures.

81   *Volapük:* A language created in 1879–80 by Johann Martin Schleyer, a Roman Catholic priest in Baden, Germany. Schleyer felt that God had told him in a dream to create an international language. Volapük conventions took place in 1884 (Friedrichshafen), 1887 (Munich), and 1889 (Paris), and it spawned numerous clubs, periodicals, and textbooks (written in Volapük). By the end of the 19th century interest in the language had begun to wane, and it was eventually overtaken in popularity by Esperanto, though it has been kept alive to this day by enthusiasts.

83   *unapproachable:* Serner uses *"inabordabel,"* a Germanization of the French *inabordable.*

89   Jamais!: Fr., "Never!"

97   bel amis: Fr., "good friends," in the sense of a ladies' man as in Guy de Maupassant's novel *Bel Ami, or, The History of a Scoundrel* (1885). A *cicisbeo* in 18th- and 19th-century Italy was the gallant and even lover of a married woman who had privileged access to her, accompanying her to public events, church, and so on.

98   au fond: Fr., "fundamental."

106   Semper aliquid haeret: Lat., from Francis Bacon (1561–1626), "something always sticks" (preceded by "slander boldly").

108   pour si peu: Fr., "for so little."

108   homme parfait: Fr., a "perfect man"; *homme à femmes,* "a man to women."

113   *Monitor the size and quality of your meals . . . :* An implicit reference to Peter Altenberg's (1859–1919) ideal of mindful nutrition and leading a healthy life, in accordance with the motto: "Aesthetics is dietetics!"

113   in venere: Lat., "in love," "in matters of love."

117 *Only someone who's been shot at . . . :* Evidently meant as a scathing paraphrase of Winston Churchill's quip (1898): "Nothing in life is so exhilarating as to be shot at without result." Serner seems to be subverting the original romanticization of battle implied in Churchill's remark with a type of behavior we would now associate with signs of PTSD (in this case, violence perpetrated against women as well as recklessly seeking out danger in general). Serner certainly had ample opportunity to witness firsthand how the war had traumatized those who fought in it.

124 *"And new life blooms in the urines.":* A play on a famous line from Friedrich Schiller's *Wilhelm Tell:* "And new life blooms in the ruins."

124 coureur: Fr., "womanizer," "ladies' man."

125 *all-purpose glue:* Syndetikon, the brand name of a viscous glue produced in Germany from about 1880 by the Otto Ring & Co. By the beginning of the 20th century it had become one of the most popular all-purpose glues in the country, claiming to work on any material.

129 *just a chimneysweep, or a charlatan:* Serner's wordplay here is *"Fumist,"* a Germanization of the French *fumiste,* which can mean both a phony and someone who attends to chimneys.

140 vieux cabotin: Fr., an "old poser," or "old ham" (actor).

150 *L.L.:* Last Loosening.

151 *To be sure, . . . :* An allusion to the well-known Latin saying: *mundus vult decipi, ergo decipiatur* ("The world wants to be deceived, so let it be deceived"). The quote has been used many times over the centuries, including by Augustine (354–430) in *The City of God* and Sebastian Brants (1457–1521) in his satire *The Ship of Fools.*

153 *these 672 fragments:* The number of actual fragments *Last Loosening* comprises is in fact 669 rather than 672. The lacunae in the fragment

numbering (82, 341, 475, 499) were present in the original, and some fragments were also misnumbered or had numbers repeated (e.g., 476 twice, the first of which becomes the missing 475 in Thomas Milch's 1981 Renner Verlag edition, likewise adopted here).

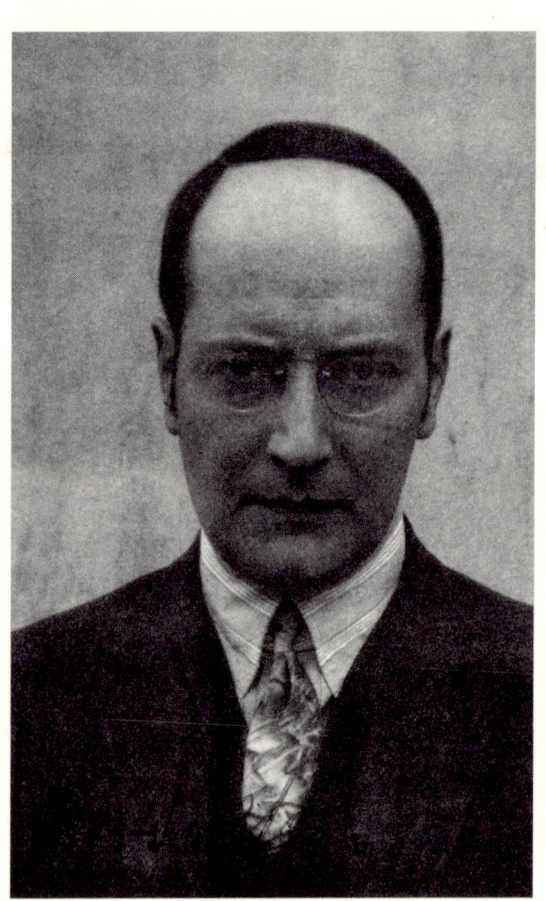

WALTER SERNER was born in 1889 as Walter Eduard Seligmann to a Jewish family in the western Bohemian town of Karlsbad (Karlovy Vary) where his father, Berthold Seligmann, owned the town's major newspaper, the *Karlsbader Zeitung*. Serner studied law in Vienna in 1913 and completed his doctorate at the University of Greifswald, before fleeing to Switzerland with the outbreak of World War I. He participated in Dada activities in Zürich, Geneva, and Paris, edited the magazines *Sirius* and *Zeltweg,* and composed his notorious "Dada Manifesto" in 1918. Beginning in the early 1920s, he began to travel and live around Europe, including Barcelona, Bern, Vienna, Karlovy Vary, and Prague, writing numerous crime stories and one novel, *The Tigress* (1925), by the end of the decade. In 1933, Serner's books were banned and burned by Nazi Germany. Having maintained a Czechoslovak passport since 1920, he ultimately settled in Prague and married his longtime partner, Dorothea Herz, in 1938. When Nazi Germany occupied Bohemia and Moravia in March 1939, the two unsuccessfully tried to escape to Shanghai. Serner and Herz were both transported in August 1942 to Terezín and from there "East" with other Jews from Bohemia, all of whom were summarily murdered and buried in a mass grave near Riga.

MARK KANAK, a native of Illinois, studied German in Zürich, Switzerland, and at the University of Illinois. A longtime resident of Berlin, his translations include *Aquamarine* by Peter Pessl, *On Wing* by Róbert Gál, and Otto Dix's *Letters, Vol. 1, 1904-1927.* He is the author of *Tractatus illogico-insanus.*

*Last Loosening: A Handbook for the Con Arist
and Those Aspiring to Become One*

Walter Serner

Translated by Mark Kanak
from the original German
*Letzte Lockerung. Ein Handbrevier
für Hochstapler und solche, die es werden wollen,*
first published in 1927 by Paul Steegemann Verlag in Berlin

Frontispiece by Leo Haas,
courtesy of the Jewish Museum in Prague

Edited by Jed Slast

Layout and design by Silk Mountain

Set in Garamond Pro

FIRST EDITION

Published in 2020 by
Twisted Spoon Press
P.O. Box 21
150 00 Prague 5
Czech Republic
www.twistedspoon.com

Printed and bound in the Czech Republic by Akcent

Distributed to the trade
in the UK & Europe by
CENTRAL BOOKS
www.centralbooks.com

and in the US & Canada by
SCB DISTRIBUTORS
www.scbdistributors.com